W9-BKD-661

Get a Jump!
THE Financial Aid Answer Book

2003

THOMSON

PETERSON'S

Australia • Canada • Mexico • Singapore • Spain • United Kingdom • United States

About The Thomson Corporation and Peterson's

With revenues of US$7.2 billion, The Thomson Corporation (www.thomson.com) is a leading global provider of integrated information solutions for business, education, and professional customers. Its Learning businesses and brands (www.thomsonlearning.com) serve the needs of individuals, learning institutions, and corporations with products and services for both traditional and distributed learning.

Peterson's, part of The Thomson Corporation, is one of the nation's most respected providers of lifelong learning online resources, software, reference guides, and books. The Education SupersiteSM at www.petersons.com—the Internet's most heavily traveled education resource—has searchable databases and interactive tools for contacting U.S.-accredited institutions and programs. In addition, Peterson's serves more than 105 million education consumers annually.

For more information, contact Peterson's, 2000 Lenox Drive, Lawrenceville, NJ 08648; 800-338-3282; or find us on the World Wide Web at www.petersons.com/about.

COPYRIGHT © 2002 Peterson's, a division of Thomson Learning, Inc. Thomson Learning™ is a trademark used herein under license.

Foreword and Chapter 1, "Saving, Searching, and Selecting," COPYRIGHT© 2002 CNN LP, LLLP. An AOL Time Warner Company. All rights reserved.

CNN/Money is a trademark of Cable News Network LP, LLLP and Time Inc., AOL Time Warner Companies. All rights reserved.

Portions of this publication have been previously published as *Scholarships and Loans for Adult Students*, COPYRIGHT© 2000 by Peterson's, a division of the Thomson Corporation.

ALL RIGHTS RESERVED. No part of this work covered by the copyright herein may be reproduced or used in any form or by any means—graphic, electronic, or mechanical, including photocopying, recording, taping, Web distribution, or information storage and retrieval systems—without the prior written permission of the publisher.

For permission to use material from this text or product, contact us by

Phone: 800-730-2214

Fax: 800-730-2215

Web: www.thomsonrights.com

ISBN: 0-7689-1157-5

Printed in Canada

10 9 8 7 6 5 4 3 2 1   04 03 02

Contents

Foreword

It was just yesterday, wasn't it—your child's first day of kindergarten? Going off to school with a brown bag lunch while you stood watching with tears in your eyes. Where did the time go?

Now, as you try to envision your child's first night in the freshmen dorms, you're feeling much the same way. There's pride. A touch of sadness. And apprehension over the many new challenges your child will face.

Oh yeah, and panic. Don't forget panic.

For parents of college-bound kids, financial worries top their list of concerns. Most fret over the price tag of a degree, which can top six figures at a four-year private university, or the complex eligibility equations that determine financial aid. Sure, you're making a worthwhile investment in your child's education, but let's face it—it's a huge chunk of change. No one's out there making it any easier. And there's no pot of gold in sight.

You've come to the right place.

Peterson's (part of The Thomson Corporation, one of the oldest and most reliable sources of education-based learning solutions) has teamed up with CNN/Money (one of the most widely respected brands in business and personal finance news), and American Education Services (AES—one of the nation's largest full-service financial aid services providers) to put your mind at ease. In the following chapters, you'll find unbiased answers to all your questions on grants, scholarships, and low-interest loans, plus tips for saving money that you won't find anywhere else.

We'll also shed light on whether it pays to pay more for a brand-name degree, scholarship scams to watch out for, tax credits, summer jobs for teens, and last-minute savings strategies for parents who are facing college tuition fees in the next few years.

You'll hear from parents who have already been through it. And you'll gain valuable insight from financial aid directors who have actually helped cash-strapped families find ways to foot the bill.

Oh yeah, you know all those financial planning tools you keep hearing about—529s, Education IRAs, and custodial accounts? We'll put those in perspective, too. Each has different contribution limits, income thresholds, and implications on financial aid—but all can help you get ahead.

Hey, with all this information, you might even be able to get a good night's sleep again.

Preface

Making a Difference: The Competitive Edge for Thinking Parents

I have spent more than thirty years directing and instituting financial aid policy at some of the country's largest and most competitive colleges—Rice, Rutgers, UCLA, and the University of Utah. In that time, I have had the opportunity to counsel thousands of families in their pursuit of financial aid for their children's education. The most successful families were those that took *ownership* over the financial aid process.

Some in the industry may claim that the process is simple. I, however, am not of that persuasion. Nor should you be. Like a fingerprint, each family's situation is unique and no two financial aid applications are alike. There are many paths to follow in order to receive financial aid, and each family deserves individual assistance, service, and, most important, solutions.

The financial aid industry is a business governed by a complicated process, and the amount of money that can be distributed to students is limited. Therefore, it is vital that you understand that you are literally competing against thousands of other families! In this competition, you must play to win. But you need to prepare yourself to win by arming yourself with solid knowledge. As John Nametz, Director of Need-Based Aid at the University of Arizona, says,

"The thinking family takes ownership of the application, understands options, and creates 'best chances' for funding. The thinking parent understands school policies: where there is flexibility and where there isn't. This mindset will enhance the ability to choose appropriate avenues for action and to influence outcomes."

The Financial Aid Answer Book is your personal guide to owning the financial aid process. Here, you will find ideas, tips, experiences, and solutions to keep your family on target for financial aid success. With this book, you will discover valuable information about the various federal, state, and institutional aid programs. Also, you will learn how a school's cost of attendance is defined and how your ability to contribute to your child's educational costs is calculated. Further, you will get strategies for filling the gaps between the cost of attendance and your resources as well as how to compare various financial aid packages.

The Financial Aid Answer Book also provides you with information that you won't find anywhere else. It gives you some of the best questions to ask admissions and financial aid officers during your campus visits. Educational professionals from across the country offer their best tips on how to keep the financial aid process moving forward. Families who have been through the financial aid "game" tell you how to adapt and best use the financial aid system. But most of all, this book shows you how to anticipate what your next move should be. You can't just fill out a financial aid application, drop it in the mail or press send, and wait. If you do, you lose the competitive edge.

The days of unlimited economic growth appear to be a thing of the past. When times are tough, you need to know how and when to get help. For student-aid purposes, you need the right connection at the right time. And this book is your personal connection to the resources available to finance your child's higher education.

—Carl Buck

Vice President, Financial Aid Services

Peterson's, part of The Thomson Corporation

Introduction
Meeting the Cost of Higher Education

Paying for college can generate a lot of stress and worry for parents, especially when they take a look at the price tags of schools. Unfortunately, many families do not encourage their children to go to college because they do not believe they can afford it. They also don't consider the more expensive schools because the high cost of tuition scares them off. Other families forego applying for financial aid because they think their family income is too high or that they have too much in savings. However, thanks to financial aid, not only is college affordable for all families, most families qualify for enough aid to make even the most expensive school affordable. *The Financial Aid Answer Book* was created to alleviate your stress and worry and provide you with the information you need to make the most of the financial aid available for your child.

This book also takes the mystery out of the financial aid process. Simply stated, financial aid is money that is supplied by outside sources to help pay for the cost of an education beyond high school, commonly referred to as postsecondary education. Postsecondary education includes colleges and universities; postsecondary vocational schools; and technical, trade, and business schools. It is important to note that there are two basic categories of aid: need-based and non-need-based.

Non-need-based aid is also known as merit-based aid. It is generally given to students in recognition of special skills, talent, or academic ability. Qualifications for merit-based aid are usually competitive in nature, and recipients are chosen because of their abilities in whatever criteria are used for selection (e.g., musical talent and athletic ability). Non-need-based aid can also be awarded based on other criteria, such as field of study, community service, or leadership abilities.

Need-based aid, however, constitutes the major portion of assistance available for higher education. When you do not have sufficient resources to pay for an education beyond high school, you are considered to have financial need. Having financial need is the primary requirement for receiving need-based aid, although you and your child have to meet other eligibility criteria as well. Whether or not you have sufficient financial resources to meet the cost of attending a college is usually determined by collecting financial data about your family and then analyzing that data according to a standard set of calculations. This need assessment, or need analysis as it is generally called, results in an Expected Family Contribution (EFC). The EFC represents the resources, in dollars, that a student's family is expected to contribute toward educational expenses for a given year.

There are three basic types of financial aid:

$ **Loans** are the most widely available sources of financial aid. You must repay them someday, but the interest rates for student loans are often lower than for commercial loans, and payments are usually deferred until after the student has completed college.

$ **Grants and scholarships** don't need to be repaid or maintained by a job. Grants are usually based on financial need alone, while scholarships are given to students who have met some criteria, such as academic or athletic merit, regardless of whether the student needs the money to help pay for college.

$ **Work-study** allows students to work 10–15 hours per week during the academic year and full-time during the summer to gain money to help pay for school.

For each type of aid, there are four sources: federal, state, institutional, and private. The federal government is the largest source of need-based aid. Indeed, the federal government alone provides more than $60 billion in student aid each year. Most *federal aid* is made available through the U.S. Department of Education and the U.S. Department of Health and Human Services. *State-supported financial aid* varies from state to state and may carry restrictions regarding residency in the state and/or attendance at a school within the state.

Many colleges and universities provide need-based and non-need-based aid to their students. This type of aid is referred to as *institutional aid* and varies by school. The importance of institutional aid has increased in recent years as educational costs have increased. *Private aid* can be a significant help in meeting educational costs and reducing debt. But typically, it requires the most work on the part of the student in terms of locating the sources of funding and applying for the aid. You and the financial aid officer at the college your child decides to attend will negotiate an aid package that will probably contain a combination of these types of aid.

In case you think your circumstances are unique, you may be surprised to learn that

$ 7 out of 10 full-time students receive some form of financial aid.

$ financial aid covers 40 percent or more of the budget for full-time students.

$ grants and loans are the most common types of student aid.

$ more than half of all full-time undergraduates were receiving grant aid by the end of the twentieth century.

$ 1 in 5 undergraduates comes from a family with income below $20,000 a year.

WHY YOU SHOULD APPLY FOR FINANCIAL AID

Here are the most common worries and concerns that parents have about applying for financial aid and why you shouldn't let these concerns stop you from submitting an aid application:

$ *The application form requests too much personal information.* With pages and pages of forms to fill out, the financial aid process may seem intrusive and intimidating. In addition, you may feel reluctant to share private financial information when you don't know who'll be reading it. Once you get started, you'll soon find that the forms aren't as complicated as they seem at first and that the information requested is no more than what the IRS wants to know every year.

$ *Financial aid is charity; I should be able to pay for my kids' education myself.* Just because you need financial aid doesn't mean that your income isn't up to snuff or that you've failed to take responsibility for your children—it's the rare family that can afford the high cost of college these days. The premise of financial aid is that students and parents should be responsible for paying for their own education, but they don't yet have the means; therefore, the government provides aid as an *investment*. A college degree usually means that the student will get a higher-paying job, contribute more to society, and pay more taxes over the course of his or her lifetime.

$ *I don't want to take on a huge debt burden.* It's true that most families have to borrow money to pay for college. But an education loan is not like borrowing to pay for a vacation or credit card debt. It's a wise investment that will produce a good return—a professional career for your child. Also, education loans often carry lower interest rates and fewer penalties than consumer loans. Finally, keep in mind that some loans can be forgiven.

$ *Financial aid is so confusing; there's too much to learn and I'm bound to make mistakes.* The financial aid application process can be intimidating. Don't be afraid to seek out help and advice from the high school guidance office, your state's financial aid agency, and reliable Internet resources. The absolute best resources, though, are the financial aid officers at the colleges where your child is applying; they will explain the requirements for their schools and work with you when you go through the application process. During the campus visit, set up an appointment with an aid officer—you'll probably find afterward that you feel much more relaxed about applying for aid.

Nothing should stand in your child's way of pursuing a college education, least of all financial concerns. Families have access to a host of programs and organizations to help alleviate the burden of college expenses. In the pages that follow, *The Financial Aid Answer Book* shows you how to open the vaults to securing as much of this aid as your family is entitled to receive.

Chapter 1

Saving, Searching, and Selecting

War or peace, economic expansion or prolonged recession, you still intend to send your child to college—indeed, you may be more determined than ever.

But in a declining stock market, you may also worry your tuition nest egg won't go as far as you hoped. Stay calm. There are factors working in your favor. For one thing, new tax rules have kicked in, allowing you to save more of your money tax-free. It's knowing where to park your pennies, how to search for free money, and how to select the right college that will start you on the right path.

SAVING SMART IS HALF THE BATTLE

Here's a look at the three most popular ways to save—Education IRAs, 529s and custodial accounts—and how they affect your financial aid eligibility.

The Education IRA: New and Improved

Let's start with Education IRAs, which have officially been renamed the Coverdell Education Savings Accounts (ESAs). Often overshadowed by the increasingly popular 529 savings plans, ESAs recently have become a more attractive education-savings vehicle, especially for families in the higher tax brackets.

The 2001 Tax Relief Act raised the maximum annual ESA contribution to $2,000 per child, up from a measly $500. And it raised the income eligibility limit for married couples wishing to open an account to $220,000 a year. If your adjusted gross income is between $190,000 and $220,000, the amount you can contribute is gradually reduced. Also under the new tax rules, you will no longer be penalized for contributing to both an ESA and a 529 in the same year for the same beneficiary.

Contributions to an ESA are not tax-deductible, but they grow tax-free. You can invest your contributions any way you wish, but withdrawals must be used for qualified educational expenses, the definition of which was broadened by the Tax Relief Act. In addition to using ESA money to pay for college, families can now use it to pay for tuition at elementary and secondary schools, as well as ancillary expenses such as tutoring or computers.

For families who count on financial aid, however, ESAs can backfire. That's because money in these accounts is presumed to be a student asset under federal financial aid formulas. Families are expected to kick in a larger portion of the student's assets (35 percent a year) than the parents' assets (up to 5.6 percent). So the more assets your child has, the less aid he or she is likely to get.

529s: The High-Octane, Tax-Free Choice

If you think you'll need to rely on aid, a good rule of thumb is to save nothing in your child's name. Instead of opening an ESA, invest money for college under your own name in an index fund or tax-managed fund, both of which minimize taxable gains.

Thanks also to the 2001 Tax Relief Act, 529 college savings plans offer some of the biggest tax breaks around. Money in these accounts now grows completely free of federal tax, as long as it's spent for higher education. In addition, contributions are tax deductible in many states.

For very high-income families who are not eligible for Education IRAs, 529s are a great option. There are no income limits, you can contribute up to $11,000 a year without triggering the gift tax, and the lifetime contribution limits to a plan are much higher, exceeding $200,000 in some states. Middle-income parents can also benefit from the tax-free compounding.

These plans do have some drawbacks, though. Many 529 savings plans offer limited investment choices, typically a handful of age-based funds, which shift investments to a more conservative mix of stocks and bonds as your child ages. Switching investment tracks can be cumbersome. And some plans levy high fees or require you to pay a sales charge. Plus, if the money in your account is not spent for higher education, you will pay taxes plus a 10 percent penalty on the earnings.

Like Education IRAs, a 529 plan can hurt your child's chances of qualifying for financial aid. Until now, the earnings portion of a 529 withdrawal has been considered student income, and under financial aid formulas, up to 50 percent of student income (as opposed to 35 percent of assets for ESAs) is considered eligible to pay for education costs. Now that 529 withdrawals are tax-free, however, experts say it's unclear whether they will reduce a student's aid eligibility.

> **Keep in mind, the new federal tax breaks for 529s are set to expire at the end of 2010, unless Congress renews them. Otherwise, it's assumed 529 withdrawals will revert to being taxed at the student's federal rate.**

In the event that the treatment of 529 withdrawals does not change, you can lessen the financial aid impact by deferring withdrawals until your child's junior or senior year of college, after most aid has already been awarded. And if you can hold off using the 529 funds until your child gets his or her bachelor's degree, you can use the money instead to help with graduate school, when aid may be tougher to get.

The Other 529 Plan

Pre-paid tuition plans, of course, are also looking like a pretty good bet these days. Such plans allow you t buy education contracts or units at today's prices to be used for tuition some time in the future. In essence, you lock in tomorrow's college costs today. Not a bad deal considering tuition fees have been rising two to three times faster than the Consumer Price Index since 1980.

As a type of 529 plan, earnings in pre-paid accounts are exempt from federal income tax, and contributions are tax deductible in many states.

Traditionally, pre-paid plans have been sponsored by individual states and designed to pay for tuition at public institutions within that state. Most are still limited to state residents, but many, too, have taken steps to become more competitive with 529 savings plans.

For example, many states now pay a minimum interest rate on pre-paid contracts, which guarantees some return even in the unlikely event that tuition prices don't go up. And some are giving full refunds to participants who pull their money out of the plans. States also have made it easier to convert their prepaid contracts to tuition at private schools and schools outside of the state.

Private schools get in on the act

Keep in mind that, unlike 529 savings plans, pre-paid plans reduce financial aid eligibility dollar for dollar.

While pre-paid plans continue to evolve on the state level, private schools have been given the green light to offer their own such deals. Under the 2001 Tax Relief Act, withdrawals from a private school's pre-paid plan will be exempt from federal taxes as of 2004. You would otherwise have been taxed on the increased value of a tuition contract from the date you bought it to the date you redeemed it.

At present, more than 280 private schools, ranging from tiny liberal arts schools like Ripon College in Wisconsin to well-known universities like Stanford and Yale, have joined a consortium of schools called Tuition Plan. By the end of 2002, parents will be able to buy pre-paid contracts good for tuition at any of the member schools. What if your child does not get into any of the schools in the network? You can get a full refund with interest. The plan currently is awaiting SEC and IRS approval, but you can call 877-874-0740 (toll-free) for information in the meantime.

Risk vs. Reward

There's no one type of 529 plan that's right for everyone. Pre-paid plans and savings plans both have their rewards. If you believe in the stock market's ability to produce steady returns and you've got more than five years before your child heads off to the dorms, you may be better off in a savings plan where you can choose more aggressive investments. You can do this while your children are young and reduce your risk as they get older. But if you're risk averse or spooked by the markets, you may find that what you lose in potential returns, you gain in peace of mind through pre-paid plans.

Custodial Accounts: Tax-advantaged Way to Transfer Money to a Minor

The new tax rules did not make changes to custodial accounts, known as Uniform Transfers to Minors Act accounts (UTMAs) or Uniform Gifts to Minors Act accounts (UGMAs). Compared with the souped-up 529s and ESAs, the tax-advantaged UTMAs and UGMAs now look less attractive. And since custodial accounts are considered an income-producing student asset, they can cost you more in aid eligibility than you save in taxes.

A potential lack of control over how the money is used is another drawback for parents. Unlike money from a 529 plan or ESA, money in an UGMA or UTMA does not have to be used for educational purposes. And since your child gains control of the account when he or she reaches the age of majority (typically 18), you won't have any say in the matter if the money is spent on something other than college.

Little wonder, then, that many families are looking for ways to undo their custodial accounts. Many but not all 529 plans allow transfers from custodial accounts, according to SavingforCollege.com, but they only accept cash, which means any investments in an UGMA or UTMA would have to be liquidated before transfer.

For families who maintain a custodial account but will be seeking financial aid, it may be wise to spend down the account before college rolls around. You can legally spend the assets on anything that benefits your child, including private school tuition, an SAT prep course, or a computer.

If, however, your child is well under 14 and you have only a small amount invested (too small to make it worth the hassle of transferring to a 529 plan), let the account ride for a while. You can then invest just enough to earn up to the $750 a year in tax-free income allowed.

> **Tax breaks on custodial accounts are modest.** If your child is under 14, the first $750 in interest, dividends, or capital gains income is tax-free. The next $750 is taxed at the child's 10 percent rate. Any earnings above that amount are taxed at the parents' tax rate. If your child is 14 or older, any income in the account is taxed at the child's rate.

Tricks of the Financial Aid Trade

As the college years approach, if you anticipate needing financial aid, strategize the timing of your college savings withdrawals, since aid decisions are based on your financials in the tax year before the school year in which the aid is used. In other words, if your child is entering college in September 2003, your 2002 financials will be the basis for aid decisions.

> **The best move is to realize any capital gains in the tax year before the one in which an aid decision will be based. And if you have more than one child in school at the same time, you should realize all your gains in advance of the first child going to college.**

One of the key strategies is to keep your income as low as possible since income is a heavily weighted factor in needs assessment—up to 47 percent of parental income is considered eligible to pay for school costs. As such, try not to incur capital gains in the tax year before aid is needed. Capital gains count both as income and as an asset—a double-whammy.

No matter what vehicles you use to save for college, be sure to regularly review your overall investing strategy. Your plan should take into account your children's ages, the anticipated tuition costs when your kids matriculate, and whether or not you expect to need financial aid.

But perhaps most important, the amount you earmark for college should never, in any way, jeopardize what you need to save for retirement. Your child can draw on plenty of resources to pay for school, but no one's going to give you a scholarship to retire. Saving for your retirement should always take priority. And the good news is a fat nest egg will not reduce your child's aid eligibility. Financial aid formulas do not take your 401(k) and IRA savings into account.

THE CATCH-UP COLLEGE PLAN

All the savings strategies in the world won't do you much good if you get off to a late start. Contrary to popular belief, not everyone started socking money away the second their kids were born. In fact, financial planners and college consultants say they see families doing the last-minute tuition shuffle all the time. If you're among them, take heart. The situation isn't ideal, but it's not impossible, either. There are still a number of steps you can take to lessen the pain.

Show Me the Free Money

The first thing to do is determine whether your child qualifies for any kind of financial aid, and if so, put the wheels in motion to make sure you get the best package possible. In 2001, more than $74 billion in financial aid was given to students by the federal government, states, individual schools, and private lenders. Much of it came in the form of grants that do not need to be paid back and federal subsidized loans that don't accrue interest until after graduation.

Many factors determine whether your child qualifies for aid and how much will be awarded, including the price of the school, the number of children you have in college at the same time, and how eager a school is to admit your son or daughter. Individual schools interpret need differently and have the leverage to give more favorable packages to the students they want the most. For this reason, it's important to shop carefully for colleges, not just for their academic qualities but also for their potential to offer financial aid or discounted tuition. It's where you apply that makes the difference.

A Penny Saved Is a Penny Not Borrowed

If you're behind your savings goal, the expense that lies ahead may look daunting. But that doesn't mean you should not save at all. A little bit goes a long way. By saving just $300 a month for one year, you would have nearly enough to cover tuition costs for one year at a public university. The same savings strategy would cover more than four years of books and school supplies for your child, which average $765 a year at private schools and $736 at public institutions.

And don't forget that your time horizon for saving doesn't end on the first day of college. In fact, if you think your child will qualify for subsidized student loans, your goal may not be to save for college per se, but to help your child pay these loans once interest and monthly payments kick in after graduation.

To make room in your household budget for savings, study your last six months of expenses to see how much you spend in a given month compared with your income. Once you know where your money goes, you can look for places to cut back. Next, set up a regular savings plan and have the money automatically drafted from your checking account each month.

When rebalancing your budget, just take care not to sacrifice your retirement savings for your college savings.

If your child is going to need the college savings in less than five years, put the money in a money market account or AAA government bond fund. With such a short time horizon, you cannot speculate on the stock market. If you have more than five years, consider investing in a conservative portfolio of stocks and bonds. And remember, don't put any money in your child's name, lest it be considered their asset for financial aid formulas.

Brother, Can You Spare a Few Grand?

Let's face it. Even if you qualify for financial aid, you or your children are probably still going to have to take on some debt. Even the most generous financial aid packages include some loans.

The most desirable loans are awarded with financial aid in the student's name and are subsidized by the government. With Perkins loans and subsidized Stafford loans, no interest accrues while a student is in school and payments don't start until after graduation. Students who apply for financial aid and don't qualify for the subsidized Stafford loans can receive an unsubsidized Stafford loan, which accrues interest during school but has far more favorable interest rates than those issued by commercial banks. Likewise, PLUS loans for parents are also more favorable than bank loans. More details on these loans are found in Chapter 3.

If your child does not qualify for a government subsidized loan or finds that it's not quite enough, consider a home equity loan first, then look into a bank loan designed specifically for education.

Your Child Can Save, Too

With all this talk of tax-friendly savings tools and low-interest loans, you might start to imagine that all parents pay for tuition. That's far from the truth. The National Center for Education Statistics (NCES) reports that nearly 51 percent of undergraduates are considered financially independent from their parents—an overwhelming number considering the cost of college today. Many parents simply can't afford it. Others decide it's their child's responsibility to pay their own way. Regardless of your reasons, there are still ways you can support your child on the road to higher learning.

> While you're looking for ways to come up with money for college, be sure to keep your child involved in the process. Would-be college students need to know that they may be graduating with student loans (consider it a right of passage into adulthood) and that good grades, SAT scores, and clever personal essays can have a huge impact on the real price of college.

Help from Uncle Sam

There are several tax-advantaged savings tools that are helpful to college students who go it alone. You'll want to make sure your child takes full advantage.

The Hope Credit, for example, which is limited to the first two years of undergraduate schooling, provides a tax credit of up to $1,500 per student subject to annual income caps for educational expenses. For the third and fourth years of college, the Lifetime Learning Credit provides a tax credit of up to $1,000 per family (or student, if he or she is footing the bill). It is subject to income caps and, starting in 2003, the Lifetime Learning Credit maximum is set to increase to $2,000.

While the ever-popular 529 savings plans are generally targeted to parents, they are useful for kids, too, who are looking for ways to make the most of money they make from mowing lawns and birthday gifts. Earnings in such an account became tax free in 2002, assuming the money is used for educational purposes. But minors who open such accounts must do so with the help of a parent or legal guardian.

> Don't forget that the earnings portions of withdrawals from 529 accounts can count against your child's eligibility for aid since they are treated as student income, which is assessed up to 50 percent in the financial aid formulas that determine expected family contributions.

Other Ways Your Child Can Save

Coach your child to save responsibly during his or her college years. In many cases, that means holding down a part-time job during the school year and a full-time job during the winter and summer breaks. Saving money earned during the college years can relieve much of the stress associated with post-graduation debt. Not only can students start paying back their loans as soon as they graduate, but they also gain saving skills that will help them throughout their lives.

When others are out partying, and your son or daughter is working the late shift, it helps to remind them they're not alone. The Bureau of Labor Statistics reports that 56 percent of students between the ages of 16 and 24 work either full-time or part-time. And many say it's a character-building experience.

Summer Jobs for Teens

Paying their way through school, however, doesn't have to mean scrubbing floors. There are a number of creative ways for your child to make some cash—the trick is knowing where to look.

AmeriCorps, for example, a year-long national service program, offers college-age kids the chance to earn extra money and even college credit. Members of the program mentor at-risk youth, build affordable housing, provide health screenings, and help non-profit groups nationwide.

Beyond the benefits of serving a community in need, however, AmeriCorps members receive a $4,725 education award after a year of service, which can be used to pay tuition or repay student loans. They can earn up to two awards, meaning the program offers them an opportunity to put a dent of nearly $10,000 in their tuition bill.

When AmeriCorps members complete one full-time term of service—that's at least 1,700 hours completed in a year or less—the scholarship is theirs. If their term of service is shorter, some members may be eligible to receive a partial award.

AmeriCorps is the only U.S. service program of its kind, enrolling more than 50,000 people a year. Its various programs have different requirements and deadlines. Some, like Teach for America, run on the school calendar and require a bachelor's degree. Others simply require applicants to be U.S. citizens over 17.

While your child serves, he or she can apply for forbearance on student loans. That means no payments need to be made during that time. Interest continues to accumulate, but if your child qualifies for forbearance and completes his term of service, AmeriCorps pays some or all of the interest that accrued on those loans.

AmeriCorps members may be able to cut higher education bills even further, however. Colleges like the University of Vermont and Northeastern University in Boston, Massachusetts, offer course credit or scholarships for participation in the program. Many graduate schools, including Brandeis University, in Waltham, Massachusetts, George Washington University, in Washington, D.C.; and Clark University, in Worcester, Massachusetts, will do the same.

> **One disadvantage of AmeriCorps: the education award for service in the program is taxable in the year it's used. But your child may be able to take advantage of the Hope Scholarship or Lifetime Learning Credits when he uses the award, providing significant tax relief.**

For a full listing of schools that offer scholarships and incentives to AmeriCorps alums, visit the AmeriCorp Alums Web site at: www.americorpsalums.org. The non-profit has con-vinced many schools to offer incentives to AmeriCorps members, whether it's by matching the education award, offering a scholarship, or granting course credit for experiential learning to AmeriCorps alums.

Summer jobs, of course, are the other option for college students seeking cash. And they've come a long way since the days of flipping burgers and mowing lawns. Interesting job opportunities abound for enterprising young adults, including tour guide posts at national parks, amusement park ride operators, and lifeguarding. Some pay better than others.

When hunting for work, teens should start by seeking out seasonal jobs. The National Park Service, for example, hires some 3,000 seasonal workers each summer to staff its 370 parks across the country and in Guam, Puerto Rico, and the Virgin Islands.

Many pay a small stipend of several hundred dollars per month with free room and board, making it more of an experience than a money-making venture. If your child is angling for a temporary gig at one of the more popular parks, including Yellowstone and the Grand Canyon, his or her application had better be competitive. Tens of thousands of would-be workers apply each year.

If your child strikes out at the national parks and is still longing to unite with the great outdoors, there are always resorts and dude ranches that cater to park tourists instead. At the 1,500-acre Home Ranch, near Steamboat Springs, Colorado, for example, seasonal workers who are 18 or older can apply for positions as hiking guides, wranglers, office assistants, fly fishing guides, bakers, and even housekeepers. Summer staffers share a variety of cabins and dormitories and earn about $1,200 per month.

Cruise ships, too, provide an outlet for students over 18 who are looking for summer employment. But it's not all fun in the sun. Be prepared for physically demanding work, long hours, and low pay, insiders say. And come to the interview armed with energy to spare.

And don't forget amusement parks, which staff up during the summer months with teens who are 15 years and older, creating a camp-like atmosphere with low rent and on-site housing in many cases. Most need booth operators, licensed lifeguards, grounds assistants, security staff, concession stand help, and ride operators. Some, including Six Flags Great Adventure in Jackson, New Jersey, even hire safari gatekeepers and wardens. In addition to their hourly wages (which start above minimum wage), employees receive free park admission and five free guest passes and are encouraged to participate in softball leagues, barbecues, and bingo. They also enjoy 40 percent discounts on park merchandise.

Six Flags awards more than $10,000 in scholarships each year to "deserving employees."

Finally, there's always lifeguarding, which pays well but requires certification in life saving and CPR, not to mention First Aid. Beach positions may be in demand, but apartment management companies tend to pay the most, offering Memorial Day to Labor Day employment to lifeguards at swimming pools throughout their apartment complexes.

Lifeguards can earn between $5,000 and $8,000 during the summer months, depending upon where they work. And pool operators, who are trained to manage a staff, operate the pumps and control chemical levels in the pool, can make another $3,000 per summer. Note that many lifeguards work 6 days a week with no weekends off.

SCHOLARSHIPS AND GRANTS:
SECRETS OF THE FREE RIDE

We've covered the many ways you and your child can save for college expenses. Now on to the ways to get free money to pay for college.

Scholarships offset or eliminate the climbing cost of college tuition and have turned the dreams of many young students into reality. Those lucky enough to land an award often graduate with little to no debt. Others get to attend their top pick, or focus on midterms rather than part-time pay. It doesn't hurt your pocketbook either, of course, since any dollars your child receives softens the blow to your bank account.

Yet, all too often, families fail to explore tuition awards for which they might be eligible, assuming their household incomes are too high or that their kids can't compete with their over-achieving classmates. They're making a big mistake.

The National Center for Education Statistics reports there are 750,000 scholarships earmarked for qualified students, totaling $1.2 billion. Much of that money comes from Uncle Sam. In fact, nearly 40 percent of enrolled college kids receive free government money in the form of Pell Grants. Such awards are granted to needy families who meet certain financial criteria. The average size of a government scholarship runs $2,001.

To apply for a federal grant, submit the Free Application for Federal Student Aid (FAFSE), which determines how much loan and grant money a student qualifies for and what a family should contribute toward tuition.

If you have questions, don't guess or leave blank answers. Instead, contact the U.S. Department of Education at 800-433-3243 (toll-free) for help filling out the form or talk to a school guidance counselor. More on federal grants is included in Chapter 3.

By contrast, private scholarships average $2,051 and are awarded to needy and non-needy students alike. Only 6 percent of college students receive them, which means the odds of actually scoring a private grant run about 1 in 17. Those odds seem slim, but they mark a big improvement from the mid-1990s, when it was closer to 1 in 25.

Applications for private scholarships vary, but students often can re-use essays. In some cases, a student can get feedback from a scholarship committee about a written application after a grant's been awarded. If your child doesn't win, the essay can be modified and resubmitted the following year.

Here's a roadmap for getting scholarships:

START EARLY. Deadlines for scholarships generally don't come due until students become high school seniors. But experts agree that college-bound kids and their parents should start searching for grants as early as their freshman year. By identifying potential awards, students can choose classes and participate in activities that will boost their odds of winning free cash.

> **To improve the chance of success, experts say students should seek out private awards based on specific criteria, whether it's athletic, artistic, or academic. In other words, you've got to work to obtain all that free cash.**

For example, a student who's achieved Eagle Scout status—the top rank for the Boy Scouts of America—would do well to stick with Scouts through high school. That's because the National Eagle Scout Association awards various scholarships, including one that's worth $48,000 and four $20,000 scholarships. Note that applicants must be a graduating senior or entering college when they apply.

Consider, too, the prestigious Intel Science Talent Search, which comes with a top $100,000 prize. Students must develop and submit their own experiments to be considered for this award. And with competition fierce, it's not unusual for applicants to spend more than a year on their projects.

LET THE INTERNET BE YOUR GUIDE. Tracking down scholarships is a lot easier thanks to the Internet. Petersons.com contains one of the largest databases available with nearly 1.6 million awards worth more than $5.35 billion.

The best Web sites enable students to submit a personal profile on line, then receive a list of matching scholarships for which they might qualify. Offer as much detail as possible. For example, someone who lists "engineering" as their chosen major may not get as many scholarship listings as someone who specifies "chemical engineering." That's because various professional groups use grants as a way to attract talent.

Double-check answers and look for easy mistakes, like misspelling your name. Don't leave answers blank. Students can modify and resubmit their profiles to see what other scholarships match. It's also smart to sign up with at least two sites. You'll find that there's plenty of overlap, but you can rest assured you've identified most of the scholarships available.

Finally, never ever pay fees to obtain a listing. There are enough free databases out there and paying money to identify grants and awards does not improve your chance of success. In fact, one study by a group of colleges found that less than 1 percent of students using fee-based searches actually won money.

THINK SMALL. It's no surprise that mega-grants such as the Coca-Cola Scholars Program and the Gates Millennium Scholars Program have certain appeal. After all, they come with big prizes that add cachet to a student's resume.

But there are good reasons to think small. For starters, thousands of students apply for big-name grants, so competition can be tough. Smaller scholarships that are worth less than $1,000 or grants from community organizations often are easier to obtain. That's also true for scholarships from local groups, such as the Parent-Teacher Association, the area Lions Club, or your local church or synagogue. Many employers even offer scholarships for employees' children.

What's more, winning a smaller scholarship may boost your child's chances of snagging something bigger down the road since it indicates that he or she is worthy of an award. You can find out about local scholarships through a high school college counselor. Another good source is financial aid offices at community colleges, which tend to be good, if not better, about advertising local scholarships.

> **A typical high school student should be eligible to apply for 30-to-40 different awards**

Beware of Scams

Lastly, you've no doubt heard that billions of dollars in scholarship funds lie dormant each year because no one applies. Sorry to burst your bubble, but that's not exactly true. Some say the rumor began in 1987 when reports misquoted a student-lobbying group that testified before Congress about employer tuition-assistance program money that goes unused. The data was misconstrued, and the myth is still propagated today by con artists who promise to track down unclaimed prizes for a fee.

Unfortunately, that's not the only scholarship scam. Since 1996, the Federal Trade Commission has returned more than $560,000 to individuals who have been ripped off by various schemes. One of the newer scams is a "seminar" where students and families are invited to hear how to win scholarships but end up listening to high-pressure sales pitches for expensive services that never materialize.

> **Con artists track down students using marketing lists. They lay on the guilt and play on your fears. But don't be fooled. As is often the case, if something seems too good to be true, it probably is.**

Steer clear of offers that cost money or require a fee. Ditto for anyone who guarantees to get you scholarship money or who requests a credit card or bank number to "hold" a scholarship. More details about scholarship scams are included in Chapter 4. You can also log onto the FTC Web site at www.ftc. gov/bcp/menu-jobs.htm. Or, if you think you've been a victim of a scam, call the agency at 877-382-4357.

Keep Applying for Free School Money

Finally, once your child is in college, don't assume the scholarship quest has ended. There are plenty of scholarships specifically geared for college sophomores, juniors, and seniors. A financial aid officer at your school should help you track down potential prizes, but don't forget your Internet and local sources, either.

CHOOSING A COLLEGE

So now you're on your way. You know where to park your savings and how it affects financial aid. You've even got some new ideas to help make up for lost time. But you're not off the hook just yet. There's still one major hurdle ahead: choosing a school.

If you plan to give your child an Ivy League education, brace yourself for the premium you'll pay. The average annual cost for tuition, fees, and room and board for private colleges and universities is about $24,000. The average total price tag for Harvard, Yale, Princeton, and their elite cousins is about $34,000. And you can count on prices rising 2 to 5 percent each year.

> One good screening tool is to seek out colleges and universities where professors have a well-established reputation for working closely with students.

Yes, college is an investment. And yes, the old adage that you get what you pay for may apply to higher education. But whether you get a higher return on a designer degree is still up for debate. In fact, some experts believe that parents' money might be better spent at smaller, lesser-known institutions, since a big part of the budget at premium schools may be used to support professors' research rather than their teaching.

The Bottom Line

Although post-graduation salary is by no means an indicator of the quality of an education, comparing alumni's average salaries is another good way to gauge the return on your six-figure investment. According to the most recent data from the National Bureau of Economic Research, students who attended a school with a 100-point higher-than-average SAT score earned 6 percent more than graduates of less selective schools. It noted, however, that students who attend more selective colleges do not earn more than students who are accepted at equally selective schools but who choose to attend less pricey, lower ranked institutions. In other words, it's the students who make the school, not the other way around, say many college counselors.

Also keep in mind that some schools steer their students toward certain high-paying professions. According to a recent survey by Peterson's, graduates of higher priced schools end up practicing law and medicine at nearly twice the rate of graduates from other schools, while moderately priced schools graduate far more teachers, counselors, and health professionals.

Job Prospects

Now, we would be lying if we said that employers aren't the least bit influenced by where a job candidate went to school. Elite colleges and universities do give their students an advantage early in their career, primarily because these schools attract more on-campus recruiters than less prominent schools. Over the long run, however, employers note that on-the-job experience matters far more than the diploma on your wall.

> **Executive search firm Ray & Berndtson, conducted a six-year study with Harvard Business School of 1,600 companies and found that experience eventually becomes more important than a person's alma matter.**

These days, the success of college graduates depends upon their ability to make their own connections. That's especially true as the new economy sputters. Layoffs, of course, do not discriminate between Ivy League and community college grads.

The Right Fit

Choosing a college isn't just about return on investment. It's also about finding a scholastic atmosphere that best suits your child.

There was a time when students relied largely on word of mouth, college fairs, and directories the size of phone books to conduct their college search. Now sophisticated search engines help match preferences with schools; college Web sites give virtual campus tours; and e-mail and message boards make it easy for "prospectives" to quiz upperclassmen and alumni about their experiences.

While the tools have changed, the strategy for finding the best fit for your child is timeless. It's simply a matter of setting priorities, exploring as many options as possible, applying to a variety of schools, and carefully weighing the pros and cons of each acceptance letter.

Before you launch a full-scale search, encourage your college-bound student to think about what exactly he or she hopes to accomplish while in school. The reasons for going to college need not be limited to getting a degree. For many students, the experience of living in a different part of the country or being part of a close-knit campus is as important as what they learn inside of the classroom.

By having a clear sense of purpose, your child will have an easier time prioritizing the many factors that make each school unique, whether it's campus size, location, academic philosophy, campus culture, reputation, or research facilities. These priorities will, in turn, be the backbone for a list of prospective schools that, hopefully, you can both agree on.

When investigating different schools, don't put too much stock in any one ranking or review. Also, don't eliminate a school, at least initially, simply because its annual sticker price seems out of your league. Even parents with incomes in the six-figures sometimes qualify for financial aid, and many schools, particularly small liberal arts schools, offer generous packages based on merit rather than need.

> **It's a good idea to start researching financial aid early in the process, as federal financial aid forms are due in early January of a student's senior year in high school.**

Another factor you should not take at face value is a school's selectivity, which is usually measured by average SAT and ACT Assessment scores. These scores are only averages. And schools increasingly look beyond standardized test scores when admitting students. An applicant with below-average test scores, for example, may get in on the basis of a brilliant essay or impressive resume of extracurricular activities. Similarly, a student with above-average test scores could be turned away if he falls short in other areas.

Of course, it's one thing to read a school's academic stats, quite another to actually see the campus. Schools have done a pretty good job of giving "virtual tours" via their Web sites. This can be helpful during your initial search, particularly if your child is considering a school on the other side of the country, but the Internet is still no substitute for real-life campus visits.

Most high school students start thinking about college visits during the spring of their junior year. Spring is when many schools host prospective weeks, in which would-be students stay in the dorms, attend classes, and even eat in the cafeteria. If you can't make the trip for a prospective week, try to visit schools when classes are in session and your child can get an inside look at campus life.

Deciding Where to Apply

Once you've done your research and toured the schools, your child will need to decide where to apply. Now might be a good time to revisit the original list of priorities. Assuming they haven't changed since the college search began—and it's entirely possible that they have—these priorities should be reflected in the final list.

Most schools' deadlines for applications are in January or February of a student's senior year. The sooner your child starts thinking of essay topics and recruiting teachers to write letters of recommendations the better. Considering that students typically apply to four to seven schools, the application process can be time consuming. It also can be expensive; application fees range from $25 to $100 a pop.

While you'll want it to seem that the decision is ultimately your child's, it's a good idea to make sure your child has applied to a variety of schools. This means applying to at least one school for which acceptance is well within reach, as well as one that may be a bit of a stretch. Also include a financial safety school in the mix. If your family doesn't qualify for any need- or merit-based aid at the more expensive schools, your child has the option of going to an in-state public school.

Although you don't want to focus too much on tuition prices early in the search, it's something most families need to consider when acceptance letters and financial aid offers start rolling in.

If your family qualifies for aid, compare the specifics of individual offers. Scrutinize each package for the amount of loans and work study you can get as well as grant aid, which you won't have to pay back.

The Final Decision

When it comes to the final decision, you and your child may not see eye to eye on the best option, particularly his first choice is vastly more expensive than his second or third. In some cases, however, there may be room for negotiation. For example, the more expensive school might still be an option if your child is willing to be responsible for student loans, hold down a part-time job during school, and work full-time in the summer. Just be sure to point out that working during the school year can take away from other activities and that the student loans could eat up a good chunk of his monthly income after graduation.

At the same time, your son or daughter might be persuaded to choose the less expensive school if doing so could free up some money for, say, spending a semester abroad or taking a cool unpaid internship during the summer.

The bottom line: When searching for a college, look beyond brand names and focus on schools that best fit your child's personality and aspirations. There are more than 2,000 four-year universities and colleges in the United States and Canada. And thanks to technology, it's possible to sift through this universe easily on line and come up with a suitable college wish list. The better the match, the better the chance your child will succeed.

Chapter 2

Twenty Questions You Should Ask on Your Campus Visit

How many times after leaving the doctor's office, have you said, "I forgot to ask about..."? Similarly, many families only remember the right questions to ask about college financial aid after they've completed a campus visit. This chapter will help you ask the right questions before you leave the campus.

The answers you receive from financial aid officers should enable you to decide which college is the best fit for you from a financial aid perspective. Also, pay close attention to how aid officers respond to follow-up questions. Look for informative, solution-oriented responses. For example, do college officials give enough detail to satisfy your needs, and do they take the time to problem-solve the question? Financial aid issues are often complex, so use the answers as your barometer for deciding if the school is financial aid "family friendly."

We want you to be a "thinking parent," so jot down any related questions that pop into your head while you read the recommended questions. The best thing parents and students can do is approach applying for financial aid with the same kind of attention as they do when applying for admission.

We've repeated these questions for you on page 195. When you visit colleges, tear the questions from the book and refer to them when you meet with a financial aid director.

SCHOOL FLEXIBILITY

The first category of questions has to deal with the flexibility of the school's financial aid office. Parents need to know how each college will treat them, especially if the financial going gets tough. For example, how does the financial aid office respond to a family's individual needs? Will the staff be sensitive, timely, and helpful when you need guidance or immediate assistance? Will a large public state university be able to assist you as quickly as a small private college? Are there current financial aid policies in place that demonstrate a willing and helpful "attitude"?

Is it common practice to apply individual cost of attendance adjustments for students and families when requested?

This should be the first question to ask in order to determine the flexibility of the school. All colleges establish a "fixed cost of attendance," (also known as a budget) that they apply to various types of students. It usually includes tuition, fees, room and board, estimated costs of books, and other miscellaneous costs. Commuting students are given one budget, residential students another. The expense of textbooks may be significantly higher for an engineering major than for a philosophy major. Or a commuting student may need an increase in transportation costs if they live a significant distance from the college. Some colleges may even reduce your expected family contribution (how much you have to pay) if you're paying private school tuition for your younger children.

In a nutshell, will the financial aid office consider additional, reasonable, allowable, and documented educational costs that are above the norm? If the answer is "yes," or if the school will review your file and take these expenses under consideration, give the school an A+ for flexibility.

What is your policy regarding "projected year income"?

Projected year income is a term used by aid offices when you request a re-examination of your financial condition based on a loss of income. For example, at the time of completing the financial aid application both parents were employed. However, since then one parent has lost his or her job or has had a serious reduction of income (i.e., stock market losses or long-term disability). Ask the financial aid office if it will consider revising the original financial aid analysis and bottom line expected family contribution and use "projected year" earnings rather than prior year earnings, which the family can no longer expect to receive. Not all schools will accept this appeal request, but federal regulations do allow for this type of consideration. If the school does consider these kinds of appeal, be prepared to prove (document) your loss of income/revenue and provide reasonable estimates of future earnings.

> **Even if you don't anticipate a loss of income, ask about projected year income anyway. You never know what may happen over the course of the next four or five years.**

POLICIES

College financial aid policies can be as different as night and day, even within the same university system. Each school may have its own institutional policies and procedures that you must become familiar with. For example, the University of Wisconsin–Madison may have various student aid policies that the University of Wisconsin–Milwaukee won't. This is important to learn, especially if you are looking at more than one college within the same state system. This section will focus on critical policy issues you need to understand in order to achieve financial aid success.

What is the minimum course load required to maintain grants?

Colleges are usually accountable to three reporting authorities—the federal government, the state government, and the school's auditor—and will adjust an aid award for federal and state aid, as required. In some instances, institutional scholarships may be reduced or cancelled if the student drops any courses. Use caution. Any reduction of course work should first be discussed with a financial aid counselor.

Most colleges require undergraduate students to carry a full-time course load of twelve credits a term in order to receive a "full" financial aid award. However, many students reduce their course load in order to protect their grade point average, hoping that taking fewer credits will lead to higher grades. Other students will drop a course with which they are having difficulty, not realizing it could jeopardize their financial aid eligibility. You must know the school's policies and ask what the requirements are before classes begin. Penalties also can be applied to students who only receive merit funds. In fact, many schools have tougher policies governing academic merit awards than for other forms of grants.

What is the school's policy on exceptions to a minimum credit load based on health or academic reasons?

If a serious medical problem develops during the student's enrollment or the student encounters other serious academic issues, will the aid office be sensitive to these circumstances when reviewing the file for possible aid reduction? Early on, you need to know the kind of personal support to expect if some health or academic detours come your way. Be prepared to document your appeal with medical records if they are health related. If academic issues are of concern, seek out an academic adviser for guidance and support. Sometimes it helps to have your academic adviser speak to your financial aid counselor to develop a plan that will meet this new situation.

May I meet with a financial aid counselor today?

While on your college visits you will probably attend orientation sessions given by admissions staff representatives. You may also speak to a professor or an athletic coach. But have you made an appointment to see a financial aid counselor? Most parents don't. The thinking parent will. You need to introduce yourself to a financial aid counselor early in the admissions and financial aid cycle so that the financial aid office can become familiar with you and your needs. While speaking to the counselor, confirm the priority filing dates for all required financial aid applications.

If you have a story to tell, this first meeting is the time to tell it. Try to develop a one-to-one relationship with your financial aid counselor. This is your opportunity to gauge what kind of a person your financial aid counselor is. How experienced is she? Will she be assigned to work with you for the year? Does she listen and understand your concerns and issues? Can she explain how to file for additional assistance? What does the institution look for in making award adjustments? Is the counselor aware of any discretionary institutional funds in the event you require additional funding?

While in the aid office, ask the counselor to review your file with you and explain how your expected family contribution was determined. Errors can be made, so you make certain that correct information is being used in the needs analysis process. If anything has changed financially or medically since you filed your application, let the counselor know. Aid adjustments can be made during this meeting. The key point is to establish a relationship with a financial aid counselor as soon as possible. Your first campus visit is an ideal opportunity.

> **Most financial aid offices, if not all, set aside discretionary funds each year to increase aid awards to students who appeal their packages. However, these funds are not publicized, and they are limited, so you need to ask about their availability.**

FAMILY MATTERS

College is financially possible for anyone interested in attending, regardless of race or economic status. But when parents divorce, the question often becomes, "Who pays for it?" Parents need to know which spouse is responsible for filing an aid application and exactly which application should be completed and by whom. Also, if a parent has remarried, he or she needs to read the financial aid instructions to determine what information might be required from stepparents.

Do you consider stepparents' income when analyzing an application for aid?

Many students come from divorced families. Financial aid issues for divorced families can be very complex. Federal needs analysis methodology requires stepparent information to be included when completing the Free Application for Federal Student Aid (FAFSA). There really is no choice here, and if you do not report stepparent income, your application will be delayed for processing. It is better to appeal later than stop the initial aid review. A financial aid counselor may be able to "override" stepparent income if you appeal (a valid reason might be the short duration of the marriage). It's not guaranteed, but sometimes it is possible.

Do you consider an ex-spouse's income for institutional financial aid consideration?

Report stepparent income for federal aid consideration and check to see what your state aid application requires. For private college institutional grant assistance, you may have to complete the CSS PROFILE application as well. Double check on your campus visit which financial aid applications you have to complete.

This is an important question to ask. Many private colleges will require this information. If the college requires a CSS PROFILE application in addition to the FAFSA, you will be required to report far more family financial information than on the FAFSA. A CSS PROFILE application is a supplemental financial aid application used to determine how best to award institutional grant funds based on need. Be sure to read carefully all financial aid application requirements. It may not seem fair, but colleges who award significant institutional funds need as much financial information as possible to ensure the neediest students receive priority consideration.

GETTING MONEY

Analyze, analyze, analyze. Your work truly begins after you receive your college financial aid award offer (also known as your "package"). You need to have a critical eye on what you are being "awarded." Scholarships, grants, loans, and jobs can make up a financial aid award. But what if you only receive a loan—should you really consider it an award? And is the school paying your full costs, or are you expected to pay a portion? This section will help you do the detective work required to keep more cash in your wallet.

How much grant assistance do you give a family that has been determined to have no expected family contribution?

The answer you are looking for here is the amount of total grant assistance (free money) awarded to reduce the tuition bill. Don't be confused by the "bottom line" answer, which could contain a combination of a grant, loan, and job. The lower the expected family contribution, the higher the grant award should be. That doesn't mean, however, that each school will give you the same grant award; even public universities will offer a different grant total and self-help (loan or job) mix in the aid package. You need to compare the total grant money against the total self-help money, as well as total cost and billed fees, school by school. Some colleges have more institutional grant funds than others and will package your aid accordingly. The best deal is the aid package that covers the largest part of your total institutional charges with grants and/or scholarship assistance. In other words, what you have to pay out of your pocket should be kept to a minimum. Certainly, there are many other considerations in choosing a college, but if cost is an important element in the decision, you must know what your bottom line payment will be.

Do you leave unmet need in your financial aid package?

According to the Advisory Committee on Student Financial Assistance, families of low-income, college-qualified high school graduates face annual unmet need of $3,800 for college expenses not covered by student aid, including work-study and student loans.

Most schools will try to convince you that they meet the full cost of attendance when awarding student aid. Most don't. What is the composition of the financial aid package? How is the school defining a "full" award? You need to know the percentage of grant and self-help assistance (loan or job).

If a school wants you badly enough, it may be willing to dip into its discretionary funds to make your college expenses more affordable.

If the school does not meet full need, sometimes called "gapping," ask if you will be expected to take out more than one loan each year. If you are offered more than one loan, proceed cautiously. Is this the school's best offer, or can they do better? This should be the time to sit down with the financial aid counselor and find a way not to borrow from more than one loan source, if possible.

What is the average debt burden of those students who graduate, and what is the average time it takes to graduate?

Other factors to consider when comparing college aid offers are total expected debt burden based on expected family contribution and length of time to graduate, which could extend loan borrowing. The average loan debt of a public university undergraduate is $15,000 to $17,000 upon graduation, and the majority of students take five years to graduate. You need to find out if the school makes every effort to minimize student and parent borrowing. Most schools increase the loan portion of a student's aid package every year as eligibility for loan programs increase. If this is the case, will the school also reduce their grant award each year?

Does your grant aid to freshmen remain constant for their remaining three years?

Sometimes the best financial aid deal is from the college that is the most consistent with its award over all four years of a student's enrollment. Don't be surprised to find your freshman year grant is gradually reduced each subsequent year, especially if you expect your income to remain relatively the same. You can be certain that most schools' costs will go up every year. If your grants will decrease, ask the schools to clearly explain their policy of upper-class grant awarding.

What if your child takes five years to graduate? Will institutional grants be eliminated in their fifth year, even if they maintain an exceptional grade point average? This situation occurs more often than you might expect. See if the school will show you typical award letters for students who received aid over a four-year period as well as for students who received aid over a five-year period.

KEEPING COSTS DOWN

There is a simple strategy to consider when trying to reduce college expenses: go to summer school. Historically, summer school was thought of as a remedial period of enrollment. But today, some of the most talented students take summer classes to shorten their academic career and save money.

Do you provide aid for summer school?

A great way to reduce college costs is to take summer classes before your fall classes begin. Ask if the school will offer any assistance with summer costs. If you can find a way to take 3 to 6 credits per summer, you can reduce your college costs by as much as 25 percent. Although most colleges will award summer loans, it may be possible to receive some small grant assistance for the summer. You also might be able to save money on books because used books are more available at that time of year. You will also save on room and board expenses if you live at home. A local college near your home may have just the course you need during the summer session.

SCHOLARSHIP AWARENESS

Many parents and students don't realize that winning a non-institutional scholarship may have a negative effect on their financial aid award. The good news is that you won it. The bad news is that you may not get to keep it. In general, a student who receives need-based aid cannot receive aid beyond the college's cost of attendance minus the calculated family contribution, no matter how much scholarship money you won. This section tells you what to watch out for if your institutional aid award is adjusted due to your scholarship success.

Will an outside scholarship reduce my aid award, especially my institutional grants or scholarships?

Every school is different in how it treats a financial aid award when an outside scholarship is received. For example, if the financial aid award from the school is $10,000, and of that, $6,000 is grant money and the rest is self-help, what happens to your overall award if you receive an outside scholarship? Will the college replace its grants with your outside award? Will the outside scholarship be used to fill in any "gap" in your need? If not, will loans be reduced first? Can the school reduce your expected family contribution to absorb the outside scholarship? Many parents don't have the expected family contribution that the college calculates. This is where an appeal should be considered so that outside scholarship funds are not in jeopardy.

Is my institutional scholarship renewable?

If you are fortunate enough to receive an institutional scholarship, you will need to read the fine print regarding what needs to be done to retain the scholarship. Make sure you know the duration of the scholarship and required minimum grade point average. Is the scholarship good for just one year? Will it increase if tuition increases, or is it for a fixed dollar amount? If the scholarship is not renewable, ask how the school will assist you with making up the difference in the following year. Will you be considered for alternative scholarships as an upper-class student?

Can lost scholarship eligibility be reinstated?

If you win a scholarship for a specific major, such as English, and you change majors, you may lose your scholarship.

Sometimes students can lose a scholarship after attending college for just one term if they fail to maintain a minimum grade point average. Quite often there are different minimum grade requirements for receiving federal, state, and institutional assistance. If you get back on track after the next term, will your scholarship be reinstated? You need to know what each fund source requires. Failure to do so can cost parents and students thousand of dollars. It is critical to be informed of each college's scholarship requirements. Determine what appeal process exists if your student has a problem with scholarship maintenance.

OUT-OF-STATE SCHOOLS

There are many rules to determine whether you can gain in-state residency status for tuition purposes. Likewise, many states participate in reciprocity agreements for tuition purposes. Each can save you money. It's important to gather all the facts necessary to know how to take advantage of both possibilities.

How long will it take to become a state resident? Do you have tuition reciprocity agreements?

Do you really want to save a lot of tuition money? See what it will take to establish in-state residency status on your campus visit. Learn what the requirements are to only pay in-state tuition. Normally, the registrar's office or the cashier's office will have the best information on this issue. There have been many students who have gained in-state status while attending the institution first as an out-of-state student. Usually there are residency committees that will hear a family's appeal. Don't be too timid to ask what you need to do. Make sure to read the school's catalog on this policy question.

Reciprocity agreements are tuition discount agreements between states, institutions, and even regions. For example, the state of Maryland has no degree program in textile fiber engineering. However, Georgia Institute of Technology does, and a resident of Maryland majoring in this field can attend Georgia Tech as an in-state resident. By not having to pay out-of-state tuition, the student will save over $30,000 in four years. Another example is the Western Interstate Commission for Higher Education, which has agreements to allow a student to pay in-state tuition at an out-of-state school if his or her field of study is not offered in the student's home state. Presently, twelve states participate in this program (Alaska, Colorado, Hawaii, Idaho, Montana, Nevada, New Mexico, North Dakota, Oregon, South Dakota, Utah, and Wyoming).

FINDING CAMPUS EMPLOYMENT

Working for a college can prove to be both financially and personally rewarding. Many students have learned how to survive their college years by working on campus. They develop a positive relationship with both staff members and other student workers. A student might also be lucky enough to work for a Nobel Prize professor in their major of study. In order to get one of the hundreds of campus jobs available at most colleges, though, you need to know how to avoid the pitfalls.

How many job opportunities are there on campus?

Ask what percentage of on-campus jobs is based on need versus those based on non-need. In other words, if you applied for financial aid and were denied, are there still jobs available for students from families like yours? What types of jobs are there? Are there any that are more academically oriented than others? What is the typical pay and how many hours is a student expected to work? It's important to ask if there is a campus employment office that assists students with finding jobs. Ask if job listings can be e-mailed to you in late summer, so you can apply and interview before the fall rush. See if the college has job listings available on their Web site. Also keep in mind that college students typically have less free time to work each week than high school students. Can you reasonably be expected to earn as much as the school has offered you?

Will my on- or off-campus job earnings affect my grant eligibility?

If you are receiving a need-based federal work-study job, consider this job over a non-federal work-study job that you may be considering. Federal work-study jobs are not be counted as a financial resource when you reapply for financial aid. Non-federal jobs are counted and may reduce your aid award the following year. In general, a student can earn about $2,500 per year before it impacts on financial aid eligibility. Another advantage of federal work-study is the opportunity to build your resume while in school. You also may be able to work off campus in a job that is supported by work-study funds.

Research shows that students who work on campus have a better chance of graduating than those who do not.

BORROWING

According to the Collegiate Funding Services "Survey on Planning and Paying for Higher Education," one out of five former college students was surprised at the amount of their monthly student loan payments. Take control of your projected borrowing needs and avoid surprises by becoming an informed consumer. The survey goes on to say that only half of parents with children ages 12 to 17 plan to bear all—or even part—of their children's college costs. If parents and students shop around now for the best loan deals, they will pay less later, when it is time to repay their loans.

Does the college establish partnerships with lenders that offer student and parent discounts on loans?

You need to ask this question because many lenders offer significant discounts. Historically, lenders deducted a 3 percent origination fee on each disbursement of a student or parent loan. However, today, many lenders no longer charge an origination fee, and they offer significant discounts on the interest during repayment. Discounts can add up to thousands of dollars over the life of the loan. Ask the financial aid office for their lender list so that the financial aid counselor can assist you with selecting the best loan for your family's needs.

Will the school package loans in order to accommodate emerging loan forgiveness programs?

Legislation is emerging that will greatly expand loan forgiveness programs for employment in needed areas, such as health care and teaching. As you progress in your academic career, stay tuned to these benefits. Your school should help you package the loans that will take best advantage of these significant benefits if they match your particular field of study.

Need-Based Aid

Let's start with the basics.

The federal government provides more than $60 billion per year in grants, loans, and work programs that provide access to college for millions of eligible students. The trick is knowing how to qualify for them. This chapter describes the individual federal student financial aid programs, with a particular focus on need-based assistance available through the U.S. Department of Education, the U.S. Department of Health and Human Services, and the U.S. Department of the Interior. You will also find out about state, institutional, and private sources of aid.

Need-based aid is the major portion of assistance available for higher education. When you don't have sufficient resources to pay for your child's education beyond high school, you are considered to have financial need. Although financial need is the main requirement for need-based aid, you must meet other eligibility criteria as well. To determine if you have sufficient financial resources to meet college costs, financial data is collected and analyzed according to a standard set of calculations. This need assessment, or need analysis as it is generally called, results in an Expected Family Contribution (EFC). The EFC represents the resources, in dollars, that a student and his or her family are expected to contribute toward educational expenses for a given year.

The Need Equation

For purposes of student financial aid, need is expressed as an equation, using two components:

Cost of Attendance (COA)

– Expected Family Contribution (EFC)

= Financial Need

The EFC is calculated through a process known as need analysis. The cost of attendance (COA) is determined by each individual school, so it varies. In general, the cost of attendance at any school includes the following items:

$ Tuition and fees

$ Room

$ Board

$ Books and supplies

$ Transportation

$ Personal expenses

A school may also include the costs associated with borrowing educational loans, study abroad, the purchase of a personal computer, participation in a cooperative education program, and a disability, if applicable.

The estimated cost of attendance at a particular school is one example of the type of student consumer information a school must provide to you.

Schools that participate in the federal student aid programs are required to make certain types of information available to prospective students. You need to carefully examine the published costs to make sure they are realistic and to make sure these costs are reasonable for you given your child's eventual career goals.

The type of school your child chooses (public, private, vocational, trade, or technical; two-year or four-year; graduate/professional, local community college, or distant residential school) can have a significant influence on cost and also on the types and sources of aid available to help finance that cost. While costs may vary from school to school, the EFC usually does not. Generally speaking, financial need increases when the cost of attendance is higher.

PROGRAMS ADMINISTERED BY THE U.S. DEPARTMENT OF EDUCATION

The majority of federal student assistance programs were initiated or consolidated by the Higher Education Act (HEA) of 1965 and are administered by the U.S. Department of Education. The most common programs are:

$ Federal Pell Grant

$ Federal Supplemental Educational Opportunity Grant (FSEOG)

$ Federal Perkins Loan

$ Federal Work-Study (FWS)

$ Federal Family Education Loan (FFEL) Program

$ Federal Stafford Loan (subsidized and unsubsidized)

$ PLUS loans

$ William D. Ford Federal Direct Loan Program

$ Direct Subsidized and Direct Unsubsidized Loans

The Federal Pell Grant, FSEOG, Federal Perkins Loan, Federal Work-Study, Federal Subsidized Stafford, and Direct Subsidized Loan Programs are need-based. Simply stated, this means that when determining eligibility for funds from these programs, your Expected Family Contribution (EFC) is considered. Federal Unsubsidized Stafford and Direct Unsubsidized Loans, which are discussed in detail later in this chapter, are sometimes referred to as non-need-based programs since your EFC is not considered when determining eligibility for funds from these programs. The William D. Ford Federal Direct Loan Program, commonly referred to as the Direct Loan Program, is a relative newcomer to the financial aid scene. Depending on which program the school participates in (some schools participate in both), you will borrow from either the Federal Family Education Loan Program or Direct Loan Program for a given period of enrollment but never from both programs at the same time.

> **These programs are referred to as Title IV programs because they are authorized under Title IV of the Higher Education Act of 1965, as amended.**

General Information and Eligibility Criteria

In addition to demonstrating need, there are other eligibility criteria that must be met to receive money from these Title IV student assistance programs. Basic eligibility requirements include:

1. **The student must be a U.S. citizen or eligible noncitizen.**

   U.S. citizen means: citizen of one of the fifty states, the District of Columbia, Puerto Rico, the Virgin Islands, Guam, or the Northern Mariana Islands. An eligible citizen includes U.S. nationals; U.S. permanent residents who have an I-151, I-551, or I-551C (Alien Registration Receipt Card); or a person who has an Arrival—Departure Record (I-94) from the INS with one of the following designations: Refuge, Asylum Granted, Indefinite Parole, Humanitarian Parole, Cuban-Haitian Entrant, or Conditional Entrant (valid only if issued before April 1, 1980).

2. **The student must be enrolled or accepted for enrollment in an eligible degree or certificate program, or other program leading to a recognized education credential, at an eligible postsecondary institution.**

   Not all postsecondary schools are approved by the Department of Education to participate in student financial aid programs, either by choice or by exclusion.

   In addition, your child must be admitted to the school for the purpose of obtaining a degree, certificate, or other recognized education credential. Students enrolled in a program leading to teacher certification from a state may also receive Federal Pell Grants, FWS, Federal Perkins Loans, and FFEL or Direct Loans.

3. **The student must not be simultaneously enrolled in secondary school.**

   This criterion has implications for high school students who are completing all or part of their senior year course work at a local college.

4. **The student must have a high school diploma or its recognized equivalent or have the ability to benefit from the course of study.**

If your child does not have a high school diploma or its recognized equivalent (usually a graduate equivalency diploma or a state certificate), he or she must demonstrate the ability to benefit from the training or education. This is accomplished by receiving a passing score on an independently administered test approved by the Department of Education.

If your child excelled academically but did not complete high school and is now seeking to enroll in an educational program leading to at least an associate degree or its equivalent, he or she may, under some circumstances, be eligible for Title IV assistance. The school's formalized, written policy for admitting such students must be met and documentation must be provided to the school to show academic excellence in high school.

If your child completed secondary education in a homeschool setting, he or she is eligible for Title IV aid as long as the homeschool setting is treated as a home school or private school under state law.

5. **The student must provide a valid and verifiable Social Security Number.**

Through the use of a database match, all federal financial aid applicants will have their Social Security Numbers verified by the Social Security Administration as part of the application process. The student's Social Security Number, first and last names, and date of birth are compared with the Social Security Administration's records. Students who fail this match must provide verification of their Social Security Number to the school to receive any federal student aid.

If your child uses a name that differs from Social Security records, the Social Security Administration must be notified of a name change well in advance of applying for federal student aid to avoid unnecessary delays and confusion.

6. **The student must check with the school you plan to attend to determine if a Financial Aid Transcript (FAT) is needed.**

Applicants for federal student aid used to be required to provide a paper Financial Aid Transcript (FAT) from each college or university they had previously attended. FATs provided information about financial aid history and were used to monitor certain aspects of eligibility for federal aid. In most cases today, schools are now able to obtain the necessary FAT information electronically from a database maintained by the Department of Education called the National Student Loan Data System (NSLDS). The new school must receive the required financial aid history information; if the school requests a paper FAT, you must comply with this request.

7. **The student must sign a Statement of Educational Purpose stating that all federal funds received will be used solely for educational expenses.**

All recipients of federal financial aid must sign a statement promising to use any funds received from the federal programs to pay for educational costs at the schools they will attend. Be aware that any federal financial aid money received is to be used to pay for tuition and fees, books and supplies, reasonable living and personal expenses, and other expenses incurred as a direct result of pursuing a postsecondary education. This requirement is satisfied simply by completing and signing the federal aid application (FAFSA), which incorporates the Statement of Educational Purpose in the signature section.

8. **The student must, if required, be registered with the Selective Service.**

Upon turning 18, all males must register with the Selective Service. This includes U.S. citizens as well as permanent residents and other eligible noncitizens.

9. **The student must not have had federal benefits suspended or terminated as a result of a drug offense conviction.**

As a result of the Reauthorization Act of 1998, federal student aid eligibility will be suspended for any individual convicted of violating any federal or state drug possession or sale law.

10. **The student must maintain satisfactory academic progress in the program of study.**

Satisfactory academic progress standards vary from school to school. Generally speaking, though, to receive federal aid your child must maintain a minimum grade point average and pass a minimum number of units or clock hours each academic term.

11. **The student must not be in default on a previous federal educational loan, owe an overpayment on a previous federal educational grant or loan, nor borrow in excess of federal student loan limits.**

If your child is in default or owes an overpayment, eligibility may be regained by paying the debt or making arrangements for payment that are satisfactory to the holder of the debt.

12. **The student must meet additional program-specific criteria.**

The following sections describe in detail the student aid programs administered by the U.S. Department of Education. A summary chart of these programs appears on pages 54.

Federal Pell Grant Program

The Federal Pell Grant is the second-largest federal student aid program and provides grant assistance to students who have not yet earned a bachelor's or first-professional degree. The intent of the program is to assist the neediest students. Federal Pell Grants may be received by being enrolled full-time, half-time, or even less than half-time. One of the unique features of the Federal Pell Grant is that it is portable, meaning that its receipt is not dependent upon the availability of funds at a particular school.

Here are some noteworthy characteristics of the Federal Pell Grant:

$ It is a grant. In other words, you don't have to repay or earn it.

$ Eligibility does not depend on the availability of funds at a particular school. Rather, if you apply by the federal application deadline, demonstrate a required level of need, and meet all of the general and program eligibility criteria, you will receive some amount of support from the Federal Pell Grant Program.

$ It is portable. If you are eligible for a Federal Pell Grant, you may use it for study at any eligible school in any eligible program.

$ The annual amount of your Federal Pell Grant depends, in part, on the amount that Congress appropriates for the program. For 2002–2003, the maximum award amount based on congressional appropriations is $4000.

The financial aid administrator calculates the actual award amount based upon your EFC, cost of attendance, and enrollment status. Because the cost of attendance and enrollment status can vary from school to school, so too can your Federal Pell Grant award.

The Campus-Based Programs

There are three campus-based programs:

1. Federal Supplemental Educational Opportunity Grants

2. Federal Work-Study

3. Federal Perkins Loans

The Department of Education allocates these funds to participating schools to award to eligible financial aid applicants. Unlike the Federal Pell Grant Program, receiving aid from these campus-based programs depends upon the availability of funds at a particular school. This means that campus-based awards cannot be transported from one school to another. The types and amount of funds awarded from the campus-based programs may vary from school to school, even if your EFC remains the same and the cost of attendance is similar.

Like the Federal Pell Grant, a student is eligible for campus-based funds if enrolled full-time, half-time, or even less than half-time, although the amount available to students enrolled less than half-time is generally more limited. Note that campus-based funds are subject to change even after your child begins attending the school, particularly if additional outside funding is received, such as a private scholarship.

Federal Supplemental Educational Opportunity Grant (FSEOG) Program

The Federal Supplemental Educational Opportunity Grant Program provides grant funds for exceptionally needy undergraduate students who have not yet earned a bachelor's or first-professional degree. Priority is given to students who are eligible for a Federal Pell Grant and who have the lowest Expected Family Contribution as determined by the school. The minimum annual FSEOG award that may be received from a school is $100 and the maximum is $4000. The minimum award may be prorated if your child is enrolled for less than a full academic year; if enrolled in approved study-abroad programs, your child can receive up to $4400 a year. Like the Federal Pell Grant Program, FSEOG is gift aid, meaning that it does not have to be earned or repaid. However, unlike Federal Pell Grants, the actual amount awarded is subject to the availability of funds at the school your child chooses to attend.

Federal Work-Study Program (FWS)

The Federal Work-Study Program provides jobs for students who need earnings to meet a portion of their educational expenses. Both undergraduate and graduate students are eligible to receive FWS assistance. The federal government provides funds that pay up to 75 percent of your wages, and the school or other employer pays the rest.

The number of hours that a student must work each week varies from school to school and from student to student. This is related to the amount of the work-study award, the hourly pay rate, or the amount of time the student is available to work.

Unlike the other federal student aid programs, there are no limits on the amount that the school may award as long as the amount awarded and your other resources do not exceed your need. To ensure that the number of hours worked is not so great as to interfere with your child's academic studies, schools usually have a policy regarding reasonable work-study award amounts. Although students normally earn their FWS awards by working during the academic year, some schools allow part or all of the awards to be earned during the summer or school breaks.

Employment can be on campus or off campus. An employer can be the school itself, the state, a local public or federal agency (except the Department of Education), or a private nonprofit or for-profit organization. Federal Work-Study employees must be paid an amount that is at least equal to the current federal minimum wage. The type of work performed as a work-study student varies. Food service worker and clerical assistant positions are fairly common, especially for students with no prior work experience. Lab assistants, library aides, and other more specialized positions are also usually available. Some schools place FWS recipients in specific jobs while others simply post FWS openings and allow the placement process to be competitive.

If your child receives an FWS award, you should be aware of the following:

$ **FWS awards must be earned, and payment is based on the number of hours actually worked**

$ **You must communicate with the financial aid office or the student employment office to obtain a work-study position**

Federal Perkins Loan Program

The Federal Perkins Loan Program, the oldest loan program administered by the Department of Education, is a source of low-interest loans (currently 5 percent) for undergraduate, graduate, and professional students. No interest is charged as long as your child is enrolled in school at least half-time. Schools are required to give priority to students with exceptional financial need when awarding Federal Perkins Loans. Undergraduate students can borrow as much as $4000 each year and up to an aggregate maximum of $20,000 for undergraduate study. Students who participate in an approved study-abroad program can also receive a Federal Perkins Loan. In fact, your child may be eligible to borrow annual and aggregate loan maximums that exceed the amounts noted above by as much as 20 percent.

Repayment of a Federal Perkins Loan begins either nine months after graduation or after a student ceases to be enrolled at least half-time. This is called a grace period. Depending upon the amount borrowed, there is a maximum of ten years to repay the loan. Borrowers who qualify because of low income may be granted an additional ten years to repay their loan. There is no penalty for prepaying all or part of a Federal Perkins Loan.

In addition to meeting the general eligibility criteria, Federal Perkins Loan borrowers must:

$ **Receive a determination of eligibility or ineligibility for a Federal Pell Grant**

$ **Be willing to repay the loan**

$ **Provide a driver's license number (if your child has one)**

Repayment can be postponed or interrupted for specified periods of time if certain conditions are met. The postponement of repayment is commonly referred to as a deferment. All loans are deferred while your child is enrolled at least half-time at an eligible school. Some deferments carry very specific conditions and some have limits on their length. Interest does not accrue during periods of deferment, and after each deferment period you are entitled to another six-month grace period before repayment resumes. In addition, periods of deferment do not count toward the normal ten-year maximum for repayment. Under other, more limited, conditions, you may be eligible to have all or part of your Perkins Loan canceled. See your financial aid administrator for more details on deferments and cancellations.

Federal Family Education Loan (FFEL) Program

The Federal Family Education Loan (FFEL) Program is a set of guaranteed federal student loan programs that include the Federal Subsidized Stafford Loan and Federal Unsubsidized Stafford Loan. These are long-term, low-interest loans available to students attending eligible colleges and universities. Under limited circumstances, these loans may also be used for attendance at eligible foreign schools. The FFEL Program also includes the PLUS Loan, which is available to parents for paying their children's tuition.

The source of funds for the Federal Family Education Loan Program is private capital from banks, savings and loan associations, credit unions, and other lending institutions. In some cases, schools, state agencies, and private nonprofit agencies may also be lenders. The FFEL Program is administered by guaranty agencies that insure lenders, with the backing of the federal government, against loss if a borrower defaults on the loan or is unable to repay it. You can obtain detailed loan information from your child's school.

The Federal Stafford Loan Program is the largest source of low-interest loans to students administered by the U.S. Department of Education. Federal Stafford Loans are available to both undergraduate and graduate students. Loans made under this program can be subsidized, unsubsidized, or a combination of both. Because the concepts of subsidized and unsubsidized loans may be new to you, it is discussed below in more detail.

PLUS Loans

PLUS loans are for parents of dependent students and are designed to help families with cash-flow problems. There is no needs test to qualify, and the loans are made by FFEL lenders or directly by the Department of Education. The loan has a variable interest rate that cannot exceed 9 percent, and there is no specific yearly limit; parents can borrow up to the cost of their child's education, less other financial aid received. Repayment begins 60 days after the money is advanced. A 4 percent fee is subtracted from the proceeds. Parent borrowers must generally have a good credit record to qualify for PLUS loans. The PLUS loan is processed under either the Direct or the FFEL system, depending on the type of loan program for which the college has contracted.

Federal Subsidized Stafford Loans

A subsidized loan means that the federal government pays the interest to the lender while a student is in school and during other periods when they are not required to make payments. Because the government is paying the interest during periods of enrollment, students are not responsible for paying the interest and interest does not accrue until repayment begins. Once in repayment, the student is then responsible for paying the interest on the loan as well as the principal amount borrowed.

To receive a Federal Subsidized Stafford Loan, need must be demonstrated under the federal need formula. In other words, when your EFC is subtracted from the cost of attendance, the result must be greater than zero for you to be eligible to borrow a Federal Subsidized Stafford Loan. Borrowing is further limited by other aid your child has been awarded, as well as the annual maximum loan limits applicable to the program, which will be discussed shortly.

Federal Unsubsidized Stafford Loans

Unsubsidized loans provide assistance to students who may not demonstrate need according to the need formula discussed earlier but who would benefit from having access to a low-interest federal student loan program. An unsubsidized loan means that the federal government does not pay the interest on your child's behalf. Instead, all of the interest that accrues is paid throughout the life of the loan, including interest that accrues while your child is enrolled in school.

Interest that accrues while your child is enrolled in school can be paid in one of two ways:

1. **Pay the interest as it accrues.**

2. **Have the interest capitalized (interest is added to the loan principal and must be repaid when your child leaves school).**

The other major difference with an unsubsidized loan is that the EFC is not considered when determining eligibility. This is why unsubsidized loans are often referred to as non-need-based. Eligibility for an unsubsidized loan is determined using an alternate need formula, which requires the school to subtract any estimated financial assistance, including any Federal Subsidized Stafford Loan eligibility, from your cost of attendance. The result of this equation is the maximum amount that you may borrow from the Federal Unsubsidized Stafford Loan Program. However, in no case may the amount borrowed exceed the annual loan maximums discussed later in this section.

> **The important thing to note here is that capitalized interest becomes principal in this process. If you choose this option you will end up paying interest on interest (i.e., the interest that has accrued and been capitalized).**

This difference in the definition of need means that unlike the Federal Subsidized Stafford Loan, a Federal Unsubsidized Stafford Loan may be used to replace the EFC, provided it has not already been replaced by some other form of aid.

Many students are eligible to borrow a combination of subsidized and unsubsidized Federal Stafford Loans. Eligibility for a Federal Subsidized Stafford Loan must always be determined before borrowing a Federal

It is important to remember that if the difference between the cost of attendance and estimated financial assistance is less than the annual Stafford Loan limits, you may borrow only up to the amount needed and no more.

Unsubsidized Stafford Loan to ensure that the least costly, and thus most desirable, loans are borrowed first. If eligibility for a Federal Unsubsidized Stafford Loan remains, you may borrow that as well, as long as annual loan limits are not exceeded.

In addition to the general eligibility requirements listed at the beginning of this chapter, to be eligible to receive a Federal Stafford Loan your child must:

$ be enrolled or accepted for enrollment on at least a half-time basis.

$ obtain a determination of eligibility or ineligibility for a Federal Pell Grant.

$ be enrolled in a school with an acceptable loan default rate among its previous borrowers.

Many schools automatically include a Federal Stafford Loan as part of their financial aid package and notify you exactly how much may be borrowed from that program. Be mindful that, unlike the Federal Pell Grant and campus-based programs, to receive a Federal Stafford Loan an additional loan application may need to be completed (in addition to the FAFSA). Check with your child's school to find out if they need to complete this application. If a Federal Stafford Loan is offered, the school usually sends the application form along with the official notification of financial assistance. You also can obtain Federal Stafford Loan applications from participating lenders.

In most cases, the Federal Stafford Loan application should be completed and returned to the school for certification of enrollment, cost of attendance, EFC, and documentation of other financial aid awarded. Although some schools return the application to you so that you can submit it to a particular lender, most will forward the application directly to the lender indicated on your application.

Annual Federal Stafford Loan Limits

The total combined amounts that may be borrowed in subsidized and unsubsidized Stafford Loans may not exceed the annual loan limits, which are specified in law and regulation. The maximum amounts that may be borrowed are:

$2625 per year for first-year undergraduate students

$3500 per year for second-year undergraduate students

$5500 per year for the remaining years of undergraduate study

$8500 per year for graduate and professional students

Aggregate Stafford Loan Limits

All students are limited in the total amount they can borrow from the Federal Stafford Loan Program during their undergraduate and graduate academic careers. These borrowing limits are referred to as aggregate loan maximums and will vary depending on whether your child is an undergraduate or graduate student.

Dependent undergraduate students may borrow $23,000 in subsidized and unsubsidized loans. Dependent undergraduate students whose parents do not qualify for PLUS Loans may borrow $23,000 from the Federal Subsidized Stafford Program and $46,000 from the Federal Unsubsidized Stafford Loan Program, less any amounts borrowed from the Federal Subsidized Stafford Loan Program.

Interest Rate

The interest rate charged on Federal Subsidized Stafford Loans when in the repayment period is variable and is determined each year on June 1. The maximum interest rate may not exceed 8.25 percent. The same terms and conditions apply to Federal Unsubsidized Stafford Loans, except that your child is responsible for the interest while enrolled and during the repayment period.

Other Costs Associated with Borrowing

Lenders are authorized to charge origination fees of up to 3 percent of the principal amount of the loan. In addition, an insurance premium must be paid that by law cannot exceed 1 percent of the principal amount of the loan. These fees may be deducted from loan proceeds by the lender. Check with your lender.

In addition to the Federal Stafford Loan limits listed above, dependent students whose parents applied for and were unable to get a PLUS Loan may borrow up to:

$ **$6625 per year for first-year students enrolled in a program of study that is at least a full academic year (at least $4000 of this must be in unsubsidized loans)**

$ **$7500 per year for students who have completed the first year of academic study and the remainder of their program is at least a full academic year (at least $4000 of this must be in unsubsidized loans)**

$ **$10,500 per year for students who have completed two years of academic study and the remainder of their program is at least a full academic year (at least $5000 of this must be in unsubsidized loans)**

Loan Counseling Requirement

To ensure that your child is familiar with the terms and responsibilities of borrowing and that he or she fully understands that the loan must be repaid, your child is required to have loan counseling before receiving any of your Federal Stafford Loan funds. Once the loan counseling requirement is satisfied, the school either uses the loan funds to offset charges for tuition, fees, and room and board or will give the loan proceeds directly to your child. The funds may be used to buy books or pay for other costs incidental to attending the school.

Repayment

Payment of loan principal, and, in the case of subsidized loans, interest, does not begin until six months after your child graduates or ceases to be enrolled at least half-time. The loans must be repaid within ten years of the date repayment begins, excluding periods of deferment and forbearance.

Deferment

Deferments allow borrowers who meet certain criteria to postpone or interrupt repayment. The deferments available to Federal Stafford Loan are similar to those found in the Federal Perkins Loan Program but, unlike the Federal Perkins Loan Program, there is only one grace period.

In addition, the Department of Education offers loan cancellation options for eligible teachers:

$ **Up to $5000 of Stafford Loans for a teacher who is teaching in a low-income school and who received his/her first Stafford Loan after October 1, 1998. To qualify, the teacher must work as a full-time teacher for five consecutive years in a school that has been designated a "low-income" school.**

$ **Up to 100 percent of Perkins Loans for a teacher who received his/her loan after July 1, 1987 and meets any of the following requirements:**

$ **Teaches in a school that serves low-income students**

$ **Teaches in a school system that has a shortage of teachers in a designated subject**

$ **Teaches disabled students in a public or other nonprofit elementary or secondary school**

$ **Perkins Loans are cancelled based on years of teaching service:**

$ **15 percent canceled per year for the first and second years**

$ **20 percent canceled for the third and fourth years**

$ **30 percent canceled for the fifth year**

See your financial aid administrator for more information.

See your financial aid administrator or lender for more information about deferments.

Cancellation and Loan Forgiveness

Cancellation of a Federal Stafford Loan is available in the event of your child's death or permanent and total disability. In addition, a portion of the loans may be forgiven by your child's participation in some national and community service programs. Ask your financial aid administrator or lender for more details on loan cancellation and forgiveness options.

Summary Information on Undergraduate Student Aid Programs Administered by the U.S. Department of Education

Program	Description	Annual/Aggregate	Eligibility	Repayment Required
Federal Pell Grant	Grant program	Annual minimum and maximum vary; for 2002–2003, maximum $3125; no aggregate	Students without first baccalaureate or professional degree	No
Federal Supplemental Educational Opportunity Grant (FSEOG)	Campus-based grant program; funds awarded by institution	$100 annual minimum; $4000 annual maximum; no aggregate (students on approved study-abroad programs may receive up to $4400)	Students without baccalaureate or first professional degree; first to students with exceptional financial need; priority to Federal Pell Grant recipients	No
Federal Work-Study (FWS)	Campus-based employment program; funds awarded by institution	N/A	Undergraduate students	No
Federal Perkins Loan	Campus-based loan program; funds awarded by institution; 5% interest	$4000/year for a maximum of $20,000. Study Abroad: Students may be eligible to borrow annual and aggregate loan maximums hat exceed the above-noted amounts by as much as 20%	First to students with exceptional financial need; must have determination of eligibility/ineligibility for Federal Pell Grant	Yes; begins 9 months after cessation of at least half-time enrollment; deferment possible; cancellation provisions
Federal Stafford Loan (subsidized and unsubsidized)	Federal Family Education Loan; funds from private capital; maximum of 8.25% interest	$2625/1st year; $3500/2nd year; $5500/each remaining year at undergraduate level; annual maximums prorated for programs and remaining periods of enrollment; total undergraduate maximum, $23,000	Students enrolled at least half-time; must have determination of eligibility for Federal Pell Grant; must determine eligibility for Federal Subsidized Stafford before applying for Federal Unsubsidized Stafford	Yes; begins 6 months after cessation of at least half-time enrollment; deferment possible; no interest subsidy on unsub-sidized loan

Program	Description	Annual/Aggregate	Eligibility	Repayment Required
Additional Unsubsidized Federal Stafford Loan—(additional eligibility for independent undergraduates and certain dependent undergraduates)	Federal Family Education Loan; funds from private capital; maximum of 8.25% interest	$6625/1st or 2nd year undergraduates; $7500/each remaining year at undergraduate level; annual maximums prorated for programs or remaining periods of enrollment; total undergraduate maximum, $46,000 undergraduate aggregate, less amounts borrowed in Subsidized Stafford	Independent students and dependent students whose parents are unable to borrow a Federal PLUS; must have determination of eligibility for Federal Pell Grant; must determine eligibility for Federal Subsidized Stafford before applying for Federal Unsubsidized Stafford	Yes; same as Federal Stafford Loan
Federal PLUS Loan	Federal Family Education Loan; funds from private capital; maximum of 9% interest	No annual or aggregate amounts, except parents may not borrow more than the difference between cost of attendance and estimated financial assistance	Parents of eligible dependent undergraduates who are enrolled at least half-time; no adverse credit history	Yes; begins 60 days after final disbursement; deferment possible
Direct Subsidized/ Direct Unsubsidized Loan	William D. Ford Federal Direct Loan; funds awarded by the institution at participating schools; maximum of 8.25% interest	$2625/1st year; $3500/2nd year; $5500/each remaining year at undergraduate level. Annual maximums prorated for programs or remaining periods of enrollment; total undergraduate maximum, $23,000	Undergraduate students; enrolled at least half-time; must have determination of eligibility for Federal Pell Grant; must determine eligibility for Direct Subsidized Loan before applying for Direct Unsubsidized Loan; must be attending a participating school	Yes; begins 6 months after cessation of at least 1 half-time enrollment; deferments possible; no interest subsidy on unsubsidized loan
Additional Direct Unsubsidized Loan—(additional eligibility for independent undergraduates and certain dependent undergraduates)	William D. Ford Federal Direct Loan; funds awarded by the institution; maximum of 8.25% interest	$6625/1st or 2nd year undergraduates; $7500/each remaining year at undergraduate level; annual maximums prorated for programs or remaining periods of enrollment; total undergraduate maximum, $46,000, less amounts borrowed in subsidized Direct Loan	Independent students and dependent students whose parents are unable to secure a PLUS Loan; must be attending a participating school	Yes; same as above
Direct Plus Loan	William D. Ford Federal Direct Loan; funds awarded by the institution at participating schools; maximum of 9% interest	No annual or aggregate amounts, except cannot borrow more than the difference between cost of attendance and estimated financial assistance	Parents of eligible dependent undergraduates who are enrolled at least half-time; no adverse credit history; student must be attending a participating school	Yes; begins 60 days after final disbursement; deferment possible

William D. Ford Federal Direct Loan Program

Despite the similarities between the Federal Stafford and the Direct Loan Programs, there is one difference worth noting: Unlike the Federal Stafford Loan Program, there is no additional separate application; however, before you may receive the proceeds from a Direct Subsidized or Unsubsidized Loan, you are required to complete and sign a promissory note.

This program includes Direct Subsidized and Direct Unsubsidized loans. You may also hear the various programs referred to as the Direct Subsidized Stafford Loan or the Direct Unsubsidized Stafford Loan. The federal government launched the William D. Ford Federal Direct Loan Program in 1994. The terms and conditions of loans made under the Direct Loan Program are nearly identical to those made under the FFEL Program except for the source of loan funds, some aspects of the application process, and the administrative details of the repayment process. Most schools participate in one program or the other.

Federal Direct Subsidized and Direct Unsubsidized Loan Program

Just as the Federal Stafford Loan Program offers both subsidized and unsubsidized student loans, so does the Direct Loan Program. Technically, Direct Subsidized and Direct Unsubsidized Loans are exactly the same as subsidized and unsubsidized Federal Stafford Loans. For instance, to receive a Direct Subsidized or Direct Unsubsidized Loan, you must complete and submit a Free Application for Federal Student Aid (FAFSA), and first-time loan recipients are also required to attend a loan counseling session prior to receiving payment.

PROGRAMS ADMINISTERED BY THE U.S. DEPARTMENT OF HEALTH AND HUMAN SERVICES

In addition to the student aid programs administered by the U.S. Department of Education, several student aid programs are administered by the Department of Health and Human Services (HHS) for the health and nursing professions:

$ Nursing Student Loan

$ Health Professions Student Loan

$ Scholarships for Disadvantaged Students

$ National Health Service Corps Scholarships

With the exception of the National Health Service Corps Scholarships, the above programs are similar to the Department of Education's campus-based programs: monies are allocated to the schools to distribute to their eligible students in designated health-care fields. Schools are responsible for managing and awarding program funds according to requirements specified by the Department of Health and Human Services.

Nursing Student Loan Program

The Nursing Student Loan (NSL) Program provides low-interest loans to nursing students attending approved nursing schools. Approved schools must offer:

$ diploma

$ associate degree

$ baccalaureate or equivalent degree

$ graduate degree in nursing

Loans may be made for full-time or half-time enrollment, and recipients must be citizens, U.S. nationals, or permanent residents. Schools themselves determine application and selection procedures. In most cases, nursing students who complete the FAFSA and any other required application materials are automatically considered for this program provided that they have need.

Schools may award up to $2500 per academic year depending upon need. This annual limit increases to $4000 during the final two years of a nursing program. The aggregate NSL maximum is $13,000. The interest rate on the NSL is 5 percent, and repayment of principal and interest begins nine months after your child graduates or ceases to be enrolled at least half-time. Payments may be made on a monthly or quarterly basis. Borrowers have up to ten years to repay their NSL.

Health Professions Student Loan Program

The Health Professions Student Loan (HPSL) Program provides financial assistance to students enrolled in specific health professions fields. Assistance is provided in the form of long-term, low-interest loans. HPSL interest rates are fixed at 5 percent throughout the life of the loan. Loans may be made to full-time students pursuing a course of study leading to a bachelor or doctor of science degree in pharmacy or a doctor of dentistry, podiatric medicine, optometry, or veterinary medicine degree.

Schools must use parental information when determining a student's eligibility for the HPSL, even if the student is considered independent. The annual maximum HPSL that can be borrowed is equal to tuition plus $2500. There is no aggregate maximum. Repayment of principal and interest begins one year after your child ceases full-time study. The loans must be paid within ten years in equal or graduated installments.

> The Scholarship for Disadvantaged Students funds are awarded by the school to eligible students in the following programs: doctor of allopathic and osteopathic medicine, dentistry, veterinary medicine, optometry, and podiatric medicine; graduate programs in clinical psychology or public health; baccalaureate or graduate programs in pharmacy, dental hygiene, medical lab technology, occupational or physical therapy, and radiologic technology; and associate, diploma, baccalaureate, or graduate programs in nursing.

Scholarships for Disadvantaged Students

The Scholarships for Disadvantaged Students (SDS) Program was developed to assist students from disadvantaged backgrounds who have demonstrated a commitment to pursuing a career in the health professions. Participating schools are allocated funds on an annual basis.

SDS funds may be used to pay for tuition and other reasonable educational expenses and reasonable living expenses incurred while enrolled as a full-time student. The amount of the scholarship may not exceed the total amount of these required expenses for a specific year.

National Health Service Corps Scholarships

This program is designed to attract health professionals to the National Health Service

Corps (NHSC) to practice in areas where there is a shortage of primary-care medical professionals. Students who pursue full-time courses of study in the following fields are eligible to apply: allopathic and osteopathic medicine, nationally certified nurse midwife or nurse practitioner, and primary-care physician's assistant. The scholarship covers tuition and required fees and provides a stipend for twelve months. NHSC recipients incur a service requirement of one year for each year the scholarship is received, with a minimum of two years' service required.

For additional information, visit the Health and Human Services Bureau of Health Professions Web site at nhsc.bhpr.hrsa.gov.

U.S. DEPARTMENT OF THE INTERIOR: BUREAU OF INDIAN AFFAIRS GRANTS

The U.S. Department of the Interior provides grants under the auspices of the Bureau of Indian Affairs (BIA). This agency administers a higher education grant program for enrolled members of an Indian, Eskimo, or Aleut tribe who are pursuing an undergraduate or graduate degree at an accredited postsecondary institution. In order to be eligible for a Bureau of Indian Affairs Grant, students must show financial need as determined by the school they are attending. Additional information may be obtained from any Bureau of Indian Affairs Office.

Some reservations also have education officers who can provide students with more information and application forms.

STATE NEED-BASED AID

Most state student financial assistance programs are need-based and restricted to residents of that state and/or attendance at a school in that state. Some states have reciprocity agreements that allow students to use their state grants to attend schools in any state included in the agreement. In some cases, state aid takes the form of financial support of the school or grants are made directly to the school but not on behalf of any particular student.

The conditions for need-based student aid vary by state as does the type and form of aid offered. A state may offer grants, loans, and/or work programs with their own unique eligibility requirements. Contact appropriate state agencies for updated information on their programs, including amounts of aid, eligibility requirements, and application procedures and deadlines.

Leveraging Educational Assistance Partnership Program (LEAP)

Under the LEAP Program, federal funds are allocated to states to encourage the establishment and expansion of state scholarship and grant assistance to postsecondary students. The federal allotment must be matched by funds appropriated by the state.

Specific eligibility requirements for LEAP funds are determined at the state level. Federal regulations authorize state agencies to extend eligibility to undergraduates and, if desired, to graduate students and less-than-half-time students. However, recipients must meet federal student aid eligibility requirements and demonstrate substantial financial need as determined by the state.

Students apply to their state agency either directly or through the school. The maximum annual LEAP award is $5000. State agencies have the option of setting lower maximum award amounts. States that allocate their own funds to the program may offer a higher annual maximum award.

NEED-BASED AID FROM INSTITUTIONAL AND PRIVATE SOURCES

Private organizations also make funds available to students and may employ need criteria, merit-based standards, or a combination. Potential sources of private grants or loans include community-based service clubs, private foundations, employers, church groups, and ethnic associations.

While the money for most need-based student aid programs comes from federal or state sources, or a combination of the two, many schools have their own resources that are earmarked for student aid. This aid may be merit- or need-based or a combination of the two and may take the form of grants, loans, or employment. Schools often receive contributions from private or corporate donors with specific restrictions attached to the use of those funds. There may be a large variety of small programs with variable requirements or a large pot of discretionary funds for the aid administrator or other school staff or faculty to award.

Discretionary funds might have strict need requirements or might be set aside to help address emergency situations unanticipated when the student's aid was originally awarded. At some schools, institutional aid might be awarded on the same basis as federal campus-based aid. In any case, you should not overlook this source of funding from the school or from individual academic departments within the school.

Non-Need-Based Aid

Non-need-based aid is also referred to as merit-based aid. The qualifications vary from program to program and are usually competitive. Recipients are chosen because of their talent in the particular skills used for selection. Merit-based aid can also be awarded based on involvement in community service, leadership abilities, and fields of study.

Unlike need-based aid, where the federal government provides the majority of funds, there are many sources and many routes you can take to find non-need-based aid. It exists at the federal, state, and institutional levels and can be found in the form of private scholarships, grants, and loans.

Whichever route you choose, the best source of information on how to apply for non-need-based aid is the source itself. For example:

> **While aid programs for health-care professionals are technically need-based, they illustrate the concept of using financial aid to encourage students to train for careers in areas of high demand. Certain federal and state programs are targeted to students in specific fields of study.**

$ Visit, write, or phone the school at which your child plans to enroll to learn more about the different merit-based programs that may be available.

$ Research the Internet and the reference section of your local library for Web sites and books that list scholarship and grant programs.

$ Check with your child's high school guidance counselor for information on scholarships.

$ Ask your child's guidance counselor for applications for private scholarships.

Regardless of its source, non-need-based aid often affects your eligibility for need-based aid. However, the way it influences other aid differs from school to school. For example, it may reduce the amount of loans you must borrow or it may be used to fill the gap, if any, between the amount of need-based aid offered to you and your actual need. While some schools might reduce certain need-based grants if you receive other non-need-based grants, the Federal Pell Grant is never reduced.

No matter what the source or type of aid obtained, the financial aid office must be kept informed of any and all outside assistance your child receives. This obligation applies even if you learn about an additional scholarship after receiving formal notification from the school of the aid it plans to offer. The financial aid administrator must take this assistance into account when awarding federal aid.

SCHOLARSHIPS

The word "scholarship" often causes confusion. The definition of scholarship is "free money" given to cover educational costs for undergraduate students. Many people, however, including college financial aid officials and program sponsors, use the word to refer to all forms of student gift aid, including fellowships and grants. Here are some definitions so you are aware of the differences in meaning when you encounter other terms:

$ Scholarships and Grants: Gift aid that is used to pay educational costs.

$ Need-Based Scholarships: Gift aid based on demonstrated need. Need, as defined by colleges and the federal government, is the difference between the cost of attending a college and the EFC.

$ Merit-Based Scholarships: Financial aid based on criteria other than financial need, including academic major, career goals, grades, test scores, athletic ability, hobbies, talents, place of residence or birth, ethnic identity, religious affiliation, a student's or a parent's military or public safety service, disability, union membership, employment history, community service, or club affiliations.

$ Prizes: Money given in recognition of an outstanding achievement. Prizes often are awarded to winners of competitions.

$ Internships: A defined period of time working in the intern's field of interest with and under the supervision of the professional staff of a host organization. Interns often work part-time or during the summer. Some internships offer stipends in the form of an hourly wage or fixed allowance.

> **Sources of financial aid include private agencies, foundations, corporations, clubs, fraternal and service organizations, civic associations, unions, and religious groups. These sponsors provide grants, scholarships, and low-interest loans. Some employers also provide tuition reimbursement benefits for employees and their dependents.**

Use the following checklist when investigating merit scholarships:

$ Take advantage of any scholarships for which your child is automatically eligible based on employer benefits, military service, association or church membership, other affiliations, or student or parent attributes (ethnic background, nationality, etc.). Company or union tuition remissions are the most common examples of these awards.

$ Apply for other awards for which your child might be eligible based on the characteristics and affiliations indicated above, but where there is a selection process.

$ Find out if your state has a merit scholarship program.

$ Look into national scholarship competitions. High school guidance counselors usually know about these scholarships. Examples of these awards are the National Merit Scholarship, Coca-Cola Scholarship, Aid Association for Lutherans, Intel Science Talent Search, and the U.S. Senate Youth Program.

$ Contact an armed services recruiter or a high school guidance counselor for information about ROTC (Reserve Officers' Training Corps) scholarships offered by the Army, Navy, Marines, and Air Force. A full ROTC scholarship covers all tuition, fees, and textbook costs. Acceptance of an ROTC scholarship entails a commitment to take a military science course and to serve as an officer in the sponsoring branch of the service. Competition is heavy, and preference may be given to students in certain fields of study, such as engineering science. Application procedures vary by service.

$ Investigate community scholarships. High school guidance counselors usually have a list of these awards, and announcements are published in local newspapers. The most common awards are given by service organizations such as the American Legion, Rotary International, and the local women's club.

$ Consider colleges that offer their own merit awards to gifted students they wish to enroll. This is a good option if your child is strong academically (for example, a National Merit Commended Scholar or better), or very talented in fields such as athletics or performing/creative arts.

COLLEGE-BASED GIFT AID

College need-based scholarships are frequently figured into a student's financial aid package. Most colleges award both need- and merit-based scholarships, although a small number (most notably Ivy League colleges) offer only need-based scholarships. Colleges may offer merit-based scholarships to freshmen with specific academic strengths, talents in the creative or performing arts, special achievements or activities, and a wide variety of particular circumstances. Some of these circumstances are parents in specific professions; residents of particular geographic areas; spouses, children, and siblings of other students; and students with disabilities.

A college's financial aid office can inform you about the need-based scholarships they can offer. Usually, the admissions office is the main source to get information about any merit-based scholarships the college offers. Some colleges have information about their scholarships on their Web sites. Private colleges usually have larger financial aid programs while public colleges are usually less expensive, especially for in-state students.

Athletic Scholarships

Whether a student is interested in baseball, basketball, crew, cross-country, fencing, field hockey, football, golf, gymnastics, lacrosse, sailing, skiing, soccer, softball, swimming and diving, tennis, track and field, volleyball, or wrestling, there may be scholarship dollars available. But, you and your child must plan ahead if you want to get his or her tuition paid for in return for competitive abilities.

> Colleges have different requirements regarding necessary financial aid application forms. All colleges require the FAFSA for students applying for federal aid. The other most commonly required form is PROFILE, the College Scholarship Service's financial aid form. Be prepared to check early with the colleges your child is interested in about which forms they need.

At the beginning of your child's junior year in high school, ask his or her guidance counselor to help you make sure the required number and mix of academic courses are taken. Also find out the SAT and ACT Assessment score minimums that must be met to play college sports. Ask the counselor about grade requirements since a student must be certified by the NCAA Initial-Eligibility Clearinghouse. This process must begin by the end of junior year by submitting a Student Release Form (available in the guidance office). You can find the latest NCAA eligibility requirements from the guidance counselor or by visiting the Web at www.ncaa.org.

But before you do all that, think. Does your child want and need an athletic scholarship? Certainly it is prestigious to receive an athletic scholarship, but some athletes compare having an athletic scholarship to having a job. Meetings, training sessions, practices, games, and studying take away from social and leisure time. Also, with very few full-ride scholarships available, your child will most likely receive a partial scholarship or a one-year renewable contract. If the scholarship is not renewed, you may be left scrambling for financial aid. So ask yourself and your child if you are ready for the demands and roles associated with accepting an athletic scholarship.

Types of Athletic Scholarships

Colleges and universities offer two basic types of athletic scholarships:

1. **the institutional grant, which is an agreement between the athlete and the college**

2. **the conference grant, which also binds the college to the athlete.**

The difference between the two is that the athlete who signs an institutional grant can change his or her mind and sign with another team. The athlete who signs a conference contract cannot renegotiate another contract with a school that honors conference grants. Here are the various ways a scholarship may be offered:

$ Full four-year. Also known as full ride, these scholarships pay for room, board, tuition, and books. Due to the high cost of awarding scholarships, this type of grant is being discouraged by conferences around the country in favor of the one-year renewable contract or the partial scholarship.

$ Full one-year renewable contract. This type of scholarship, which has basically replaced the four-year grant, is automatically renewed at the end of each school year for four years if the conditions of the contract are met. The recruiter will probably tell your child in good faith that the intent is to offer a four-year scholarship, but he is legally only allowed to offer you a one-year grant. You must ask the recruiter as well as other players what the record has been of renewing scholarships for athletes who comply athletically, academically, and socially.

$ One-year trial grant (full or partial). This is a verbal agreement between the student and the institution that at the end of the year. Renewal is dependent upon the student's academic and athletic performance.

$ Partial scholarship. The partial grant is any part of the total cost of college. The student may be offered room and board but not tuition and books. Or he or she may be offered just tuition. The possibility exists to negotiate to a full scholarship after the freshman year.

$ Waiver of out-of-state fees. This award is for out-of-state students to attend a college or university at the same fee as an in-state student.

Finding and Getting Athletic Scholarships

Here are four steps to help your child snag that scholarship:

1. **Contact the school formally.** Once your child has made a list of schools he or she is interested in, get the name of the head coach and have your child write a letter to the top twenty schools on the list. Then compile a factual resume of his or her athletic and academic accomplishments. Put together 10–15 minutes of video highlights of his or her athletic performance (with the player's jersey number noted), get letters of recommendation from his or her high school coach and off-season coach, and include a season schedule.

2. **Ace the interview.** Before your child meets a recruiter or coach, stress to him or her the importance of exhibiting self-confidence by using a firm handshake, maintaining eye contact, and making sure that the student is well groomed. According to recruiters, the most effective attitude is quiet confidence, respect, sincerity, and enthusiasm.

3. **Ask good questions.** Don't be afraid to probe the recruiter by getting answers to the following questions: Does my child qualify athletically and academically? If he or she is recruited, what would the parameters of the scholarship be? For what position is he or she being considered? It's okay to ask the recruiter to declare what level of interest he or she has in your child.

4. **Follow up.** Persistence pays off when it comes to seeking an athletic scholarship. And timing can be everything. There are four good times when a follow-up letter from a coach or a personal letter from the student is extremely effective. These are prior to the senior season, during or just after the senior season, just prior to or after announced signing dates (conference-affiliated or national association), and late summer, in case scholarship offers have been withdrawn or declined.

To sum up, look at your child's skills objectively, both athletic and academic. Evaluate those skills that need improvement and keep your child's desire to improve alive. Help your child to develop his or her leadership skills and keep striving for excellence with his or her individual achievements.

STATE AND LOCAL SCHOLARSHIPS

Each state government has established one or more financial aid programs for qualified students. Usually, only legal residents of the state are eligible to benefit from such programs. However, some are available to out-of-state students attending colleges within the state. States may also offer internship or work-study programs, graduate fellowships and grants, or low-interest loans in addition to grant and forgivable loan programs.

> **Ask your child's coach or assistant coaches for recommendations; learn about the conference or institution from newspaper or television coverage; ask your child's guidance counselor; review guidebooks, reference books, and the Internet; ask alumni; or attend a tryout or campus visit. You can also write to the NCAA to request a recruiting guide for your sport.**

Many states are trying to encourage students to enter specific occupational fields where a shortage of trained personnel exists. Examples are education, science, nursing, and medicine. To attract individuals to these fields, more and more states now provide special loan assistance to students who promise to work in these areas after graduation. If your child accepts such assistance, he or she should confirm whether there is a service obligation as part of the award.

If you are interested in learning more about state-sponsored programs, the state higher education office should be able to provide information. Brochures and application forms for state scholarship programs are usually available in your child's high school guidance office or from a college financial aid office in your state. Increasingly, state government agencies are putting state scholarship information on their Web sites. The financial aid page of state-administered college or university sites frequently has a list of state-sponsored scholarships and financial aid programs.

Businesses, community service clubs, and local organizations often sponsor scholarship programs for residents of a specific town or county.

These can be attractive to a scholarship seeker because the odds of winning can be higher than they would be for scholarships drawing from a wider pool of applicants. However, because the information network at the local level is spotty, it is often difficult to find information about their existence. Some of the best sources of information about these local programs are high school guidance offices, community college financial aid offices, high school district administrative offices, and public libraries.

PRIVATE AID

Billions of dollars every year are given by private donors to students and their families to help with the expenses of a college education. Last year, non-institutional and non-government sponsors gave more than $3 billion in financial aid to help undergraduate students pay for college costs. Foundations, fraternal and ethnic organizations, community service clubs, churches and religious groups, philanthropies, companies and industry groups, labor unions and public employees' associations, veterans' groups, trusts, and bequests all make up a large network of possible sources.

In addition, you may want to check with the local offices of organizations that traditionally sponsor scholarships, such as the International Kiwanis Club, the Benevolent and Protective Order of Elks, the Lions Club International, or the National Association of American Business Clubs (AMBUCS).

It is always worthwhile for any prospective student to look into these scholarships. It is especially important for students who do not qualify for need-based financial aid, students and families who wish to supplement the aid being given by governmental or university sources, and students who possess special abilities, achievements, or personal qualifications (e.g., memberships in church or civic organizations, specific ethnic backgrounds, parents who served in the armed forces, etc.) that fit the criteria of one or more of the various private scholarship sponsors.

Some factors that can affect eligibility for these awards are beyond your control, such as ethnic heritage and parental status. Other factors, such as academic, scientific, technological, athletic, artistic, or creative merit, are not easily or quickly met unless the student has previously committed to a particular endeavor. However, eligibility for many programs is within your control if you plan ahead. For example, your child can start or keep up current membership in a church or civic organization, participate in volunteer service efforts, or pursue an interest, from amateur radio to golf to raising animals to writing and more. Any of these actions might give him or her an edge for a particular scholarship or grant opportunity.

The eligibility criteria for private scholarships, grants, and prizes vary widely and include financial need as well as personal characteristics and merit. The number and amounts of the awards available from individual sponsors can vary each year depending upon the number of grantees, fund contributions, and other factors. However, practically anyone can find awards to fit his or her individual circumstances.

The Scholarship Game: A Strategic Approach

Before you start off on your odyssey for scholarships, keep in mind these general insights, strategies, and observations about the scholarship game:

$ **Start early.** It is highly advisable to start entering contests early in your child's high school career. There are even a number of programs that include separate competitions for grades 7–9. In many of the largest scholarship competitions, students who have not won a top prize can enter each year that they are eligible. For experience alone, it is worthwhile to get involved as a freshman or sophomore.

$ **Begin preparing in advance.** To achieve success in national scholarship contests, it is wise to begin your preparation with time to spare before the deadlines start creeping up. Areas such as writing and the arts, participants may be required to submit large portfolios of work. Several programs in math and science involve complex, time-consuming projects. Students hoping to win honors in public speaking contests usually benefit from repeated practice. Early preparation is a definite mark of a competitive entrant.

$ **The Minuteman approach.** Be ready for whatever opportunities may become available. If your child is a senior, it's a good idea to keep a file of materials that are often required. By holding on to copies of papers and documents, you can quickly duplicate them and send them off as part of scholarship application forms without wasting valuable time. Keep copies of at least three recommendations on file (from the principal or vice-principal, guidance counselor, and one or more teachers) concerning your child's academic and nonacademic achievements as well as his or her personal qualities. Keep copies of any general college application essays written that can be recycled for scholarship application forms. If your child has a number of impressive achievements in a certain area (debate victories, athletic awards, published newspaper articles, etc.), list and describe them in a one-page write-up that can be added to scholarship forms. If your child is interested in entering writing competitions, keep typewritten copies on hand of his or her best work. Program deadlines do not always fall at convenient moments. Time is money—scholarship money.

$ **Obtain and examine past winning entries.** Winners of scholarships in writing or public speaking have often benefited from studying the entries of previous contest winners. Examples can usually be obtained by writing directly to the contest administrators.

$ **Make friends with your guidance counselor.** Have your child talk with his or her counselor at the beginning of the school year and request assistance in your efforts to enter and win competitions. Get copies of all information that the school receives about scholarship opportunities in fields that interest your child.

$ **The "Spillover Effect."** Entering scholarship competitions isn't as much work as it appears to be. Students can make their intellectual and creative efforts work overtime for them. You may find that several contests in one field—such as science, public speaking, the arts, or writing— have similar requirements, and work that was prepared for one contest can be adapted for use in several others.

$ **The "Success leads to success" syndrome.** There is a definite cumulative effect in winning competitive awards.

Success in performance-oriented competitions forms an impressive background of past achievements when applying for the next competition.

$ **Use original material only.** Plagiarism is the fastest way to be eliminated from a program. Be certain that your child submits his or her own work or gives appropriate credit to material taken from other sources.

$ **Read all contest materials carefully.** Although this seems obvious, numerous contest officials have pointed out that many students do not pay attention to the rules. Be sure to obtain a copy of the most recent brochure to get firsthand information about deadlines, correct entry procedures, and scholarship criteria. Don't take someone else's word about contest rules, even that of a well-meaning friend or school adviser.

VETERANS EDUCATIONAL BENEFITS

The Department of Veterans Affairs and the Department of Defense administer several educational assistance programs for veterans and their dependents.

The Survivors and Dependents Educational Assistance Program (DEAP) provides benefits to children and spouses of veterans who died or were permanently disabled as a result of a service-related injury. Under the DEAP, dependents between the ages of 18 and 26 may receive a stipend (prorated for less-than-full-time enrollment) at the completion of each month of study. This monthly stipend from the Department of Veterans Affairs helps to cover educational and personal expenses that are incurred while the student is enrolled at a post-secondary school. Note that these benefits must be considered as a resource by the aid administrator when a student's eligibility for federal, state, and institutional assistance is determined.

Veterans' benefits are paid to students for the following types of education programs:

$ Undergraduate and graduate degree programs

$ Cooperative training programs

$ Accredited independent study programs leading to a college degree

$ Courses leading to a certificate or diploma from business, technical, or vocational schools

$ Apprenticeships or job training programs offered by a company or union

$ Farm cooperative courses

$ Study-abroad programs that lead to a college degree

Additional information regarding these and other veterans' educational benefits may be obtained from the nearest office of the Department of Veterans Affairs or by accessing their Web site at www.va.gov. You also can call or write the nearest VA office for pamphlets and brochures.

VOCATIONAL REHABILITATION FOR THE DISABLED

Access to educational opportunity for individuals with disabilities is guaranteed through federal laws governing vocational rehabilitation. Federal allocations are provided to each state on a matching basis to assist people with disabilities who have employment potential but whose impairments create barriers to that employment.

Vocational rehabilitation programs also provide comprehensive services under an individualized written rehabilitation plan. The plan can include evaluation, vocational training, special devices required for employment, job placement, and follow-up services. Some states offer educational assistance programs to disabled students through agencies that are often known as Offices of Vocational Rehabilitation (OVR). While students with disabilities may participate in any of the federal financial aid programs, additional aid through vocational rehabilitation programs can be used to pay for unique expenses incurred due to a disability. Eligible students can also receive funds for tuition, fees, books and supplies, and maintenance and transportation allowances.

If your child is disabled, contact your state department of vocational rehabilitation for further information. You can also obtain information related to both aid and access from HEATH, a clearinghouse funded by the U.S. Department of Education and maintained by the American Council on Education (ACE). HEATH's contact information is:

One Dupont Circle, NW

Suite 800, Washington, D.C. 20036-1193

Telephone: 202-939-9320 or 800-544-3284 (toll free)

SCHOLARSHIP SCAMS: WHAT THEY ARE AND WHAT TO WATCH OUT FOR

An award from a private source can tilt the scales with respect to a student's ability to attend a specific college during a particular year. Unfortunately for prospective scholarship seekers, there are few patterns or rules for the private aid sector. It is a mix of individual programs, each with its own award criteria, timetables, application procedures, and decision-making processes. Considerable effort is required to understand and effectively benefit from private scholarships.

Unfortunately, the combination of a sharp urgency to locate money, limited time, and this complex system has created opportunities for fraud. For every ten students who receive a legitimate scholarship, one is victimized by a fraudulent scheme or scam that poses as a legitimate foundation, scholarship sponsor, or scholarship search service.

These fraudulent businesses advertise in campus newspapers, distribute flyers, mail letters and postcards, provide toll-free phone numbers, and even have sites on the World Wide Web. The most obvious frauds operate as scholarship search services or scholarship clearinghouses. A less obvious example is a business set up as a scholarship sponsor. It pockets the money from the fees and charges that are paid by thousands of hopeful scholarship seekers, and returns little, if anything, in proportion to the amounts it collects. A few of these frauds inflict great harm by gaining access to individuals' credit or checking accounts with the intent to extort funds.

A typical mode of operation for a fraudulent firm is to send out a huge mailing (more than a million postcards each year for some outfits) to college and high school students claiming that the company has either a scholarship or a scholarship list for the students. These companies often provide toll-free numbers. When recipients call, they are told by high-pressure telemarketers that the company has unclaimed scholarships and that for fees ranging from $10 to $400 the callers get back at least $1,000 in scholarship money or the fee will be refunded. Customers who pay may not receive anything at all or are sometimes mailed a list of sources of financial aid that are no better than or inferior to what can be found in any of the major scholarship guides available in bookstores or libraries. The "lucky" recipients have to apply on their own for the scholarships. Many of the programs are contests, loans, or work-study programs rather than gift aid. Some are no longer in existence, have expired deadlines, or demand eligibility requirements that the students cannot meet. Customers who seek refunds have to demonstrate that they have applied in writing to each source on the list and received a rejection letter from each of them. Frequently, even when customers can provide this almost-impossible-to-obtain proof, refunds are not made. In the worst cases, the companies ask for students' checking account or credit card numbers and take funds without authorization.

There are some legitimate scholarship search services. However, a scholarship search service cannot truthfully guarantee that a student will receive a scholarship, and students are better off doing their own homework using a reliable scholarship information source than by wasting money, and sometimes more important, time, with a search service that promises a scholarship.

The FTC warns scholarship seekers to be alert for these six warning signs of a scam:

1. **"This scholarship is guaranteed or your money back."** No service can guarantee that it will get your child a grant or scholarship. Refund guarantees often have impossible conditions attached. Review a service's refund policies in writing before you pay a fee. Typically, fraudulent scholarship search services require that applicants show rejection letters from each of the sponsors on the list they provide. If a sponsor no longer exists, if it really does not provide scholarships, or if it has a rolling application deadline, letters of rejection are almost impossible to obtain.

The FTC warns students and their parents to be wary of fraudulent search services that promise to do all the work for you. "Bogus scholarship search services are just a variation on the 'you have won' prize-promotion scam, targeted to a particular audience—students and their parents who are anxious about paying for college," said Jodie Bernstein, Director of the FTC's Bureau of Consumer Protection. "They guarantee students and their families free scholarship money . . . all they have to do to claim it is pay an up-front fee."

2. "The scholarship service will do all the work." Unfortunately, nobody else can fill out the personal information forms, write the essays, and supply the references that many scholarships may require.

3. "The scholarship will cost some money." Be wary of any charges related to scholarship information services or individual scholarship applications, especially in significant amounts. Some legitimate scholarship sponsors charge fees to defray their processing expenses. True scholarship sponsors, however, should give out money, not make it from application fees. Before you send money to apply for a scholarship, investigate the sponsor.

4. "You can't get this information anywhere else." Scholarship directories from many publishers are available in any large bookstore, public library, or high school guidance office.

5. **"You are a finalist—in a contest you never entered," or "You have been selected by a national foundation to receive a scholarship."** Most legitimate scholarship programs almost never seek particular applicants. Most scholarship sponsors will only contact you in response to an inquiry. Most lack the budget and mandate to do anything more than this. Should you think that there is any real possibility that your child may have been selected to receive a scholarship, before you send any money, investigate first to be sure that the sponsor or program is legitimate.

6. **"The scholarship service needs your credit card or checking account number in advance."** Never provide your credit card or bank account number on the telephone to the representative of an organization that you do not know. A legitimate need-based scholarship program will not ask for your checking account number. Get information in writing first. An

unscrupulous operation does not need your signature on a check. It schemes to set up situations that allow it to drain a victim's account with unauthorized withdrawals.

In addition to the FTC's six signs, here are some other points to keep in mind when considering a scholarship program:

$ Fraudulent scholarship operations often use official-sounding names containing words such as federal, national, administration, division, federation, and foundation. Their names often are a slight variant of the name of a legitimate government or private organization. Do not be fooled by a name that seems reputable or official, an official-looking seal, or a Washington, D.C. address.

$ If your child wins a scholarship, he or she will receive written official notification by mail not by telephone. If the sponsor calls to inform you, it will follow up with a letter in the mail. If a request for money is made by phone, the operation is probably fraudulent.

$ Be wary if an organization's address is a box number or a residential address. If a bona fide scholarship program uses a post office box number, it usually will include a street address and telephone number on its stationery.

$ Beware of telephone numbers with a 900 area code. These may charge you a fee of several dollars a minute for a call that could be a long recording that provides only a list of addresses or names.

$ A dishonest operation may put pressure on an applicant by saying that awards are on a first-come, first-served basis. Some scholarship programs give preference to the earlier qualified applications. However, if you are told, especially on the telephone, that you must respond quickly, but you will not hear about the results for several months, there may be a problem.

$ Be wary of endorsements. Fraudulent operations claim endorsements by groups with names similar to well-known private or government organizations. The Better Business Bureau (BBB) and government agencies do not endorse businesses.

If an organization requires you to pay money for a scholarship that you have never heard of before and you cannot verify that it is a legitimate operation, the best advice is not to pay anything. If you have already paid money to such an organization and find reason to doubt its legitimacy, call your bank to stop payment on your check, if possible, or call your credit card company and tell it that you think you were the victim of a consumer fraud.

There are many wonderful scholarships available to qualified students who spend the time and effort to locate and apply for them. But exercise caution in using scholarship search services and, when you must pay money, practice careful judgment in considering a scholarship program's sponsor.

To find out how to recognize, report, and stop a scholarship scam, contact:

The Federal Trade Commission
600 Pennsylvania Avenue, NW
Washington, D.C. 20580
www.ftc.gov

The National Fraud Information Center
www.fraud.org
(800) 876-7060

The Council of Better Business Bureaus
4200 Wilson Boulevard, Suite 800
Arlington, Virginia 22203-1838
(703) 276-0100 (call to get a telephone number of your local BBB office and the BBB office in the area the organization in question is located)
www.bbb.org (this has a directory of local offices and complaint forms)

Chapter 5

101 Tips from the Pros

Securing financial aid is a complicated and daunting process. Knowing someone who deals with the topic every day can make it a lot less frightening. So Peterson's recently surveyed education professionals to find out what they think are the most important things families need to know about financial aid. We've gathered their top 101 tips in this chapter to put you on a level playing field with the financial aid officers at the schools your child is applying to.

PREPARATION AND FACT-FINDING— PARENTS

1. **Talk with your child about your ability and willingness to pay for college.** Keep the lines of communication open about finances. Parents and students who don't discuss finances as part of the college selection process often have a difficult time when a student's first-choice college turns out to be the one the parents can't afford. Be clear and realistic about your financial limitations as well as your expectations of the role your child will take in the process and in financing.

2. **Find out how much college "really" costs.** A figure that continually appears in the media is $30,000 a year. But just as the cost of an automobile depends on the make and model, college costs can vary widely. If your son or daughter attends a

local community college and lives at home, your out-of-pocket costs for the entire academic year may only be a few thousand dollars. A state-supported public university will have a total cost of education anywhere from $10,000 to $17,000 a year. An Ivy League college education can easily cost $37,000 annually. (These costs are for the nine-month academic year and include tuition and fees, books and supplies, transportation expenses, room and board, etc.)

3. **Everyone should apply for financial aid.** There are so many different factors that determine aid eligibility that no one can give you a simple answer as to whether or not you are eligible for aid. Family income and assets are not the only aspects that determine eligibility for need-based aid; family size and number of children in college are almost as important.

4. **Parents should make sure students are involved in and understand the financial aid process.** At most schools, the student is the first point of contact for administrative issues. In addition, many times the financial aid process is the first step that students take in learning to manage their own financial matters.

5. **Parents should complete a sample Free Application for Federal Student Aid (FAFSA) when the student becomes a junior in high school.** This will give you an idea of what your Expected Family Contribution (EFC) will be. The results can assist you in selecting affordable colleges. This can be done at most high school career centers or by using any of the Need Analysis Calculators on the Internet. (See www.petersons.com)

6. **If you haven't started any kind of savings for college, start putting some money aside now.** The money you put in the bank today can be used as a resource for college. More importantly, you have created an on-going resource in your family budget that can be used for a loan payment or monthly payment plan when your child is in college.

7. **Invest in a Qualified State Tuition Plan (QSTP), more commonly referred to as an I-529 Plan. (Derived from Internal Revenue Service Code I-529.)** There are two types of plans under I-529. The Prepaid College Tuition Plan allows for investors to invest funds in a state plan that freezes the cost of tuition at the present rate and guarantees against tuition inflation in the future. The second is the College Investment Plan, which allows investors (sponsors) to invest in a I-529 plan at any point they wish to contribute. There is no guarantee on meeting tuition costs, but there are many benefits when participating in a state-sponsored college investment plan, including state income tax deductions, federal tax-free earnings, tax-deferred savings, and exemption of listing this asset as a student asset on the FAFSA. Many states give tax benefits at the state level as well as federal tax-free benefits when funds are used for college students. Prepaid tuition plans are exempt from being listed on the FAFSA, but the College Investment Plan is not.

8. **Ask your employer(s), union, and any community clubs to which you belong if they offer financial aid to students.**

9. **Investigate scholarship search services.** If your child is an exceptional student and you feel she might qualify for academic scholarship recognition, there are many free scholarship search services available, such as Peterson's (www.petersons.com). You never need to pay for such assistance.

10. **Investigate PLUS loans.** If you have sufficient resources to finance your child's college costs but are concerned that you may not have enough cash on hand for all those expenses, the federal government has created a non-need-based loan program—the Parent Loan for Undergraduate Students (PLUS). All families can take advantage of this program regardless of current income. While it is important to remember that this program is a loan, it is nevertheless available to all parents regardless of income and currently is at a historically low interest rate (4.86%). Through the PLUS loan program, you can borrow up to the full cost of education less any financial aid awarded.

11. **Reduce your child's savings.** If you have shifted significant resources into your children's names to lessen your federal income tax burden, this could reduce your children's financial aid eligibility. In the calculations for financial aid eligibility, the student's savings are taxed at a much higher rate than those savings reported for parents. If you or your child have set aside funds for college expenses, consider using those savings to pay for necessary college expenses—perhaps a new vehicle or prepayment of tuition and fees—from those savings prior to filling out the needs analysis form. It might make a significant difference, particularly if those expenditures reduce the student's savings.

12. **Be careful about listening to neighbors and friends who tell you what to do or what will happen.** Unless you see their tax return or bank statement, you really don't know much about their finances. You only see how they spent their money.

PREPARATION AND FACT-FINDING— STUDENTS

13. **Listen when your parents talk with you about financing.** This is big bucks!

14. **View your education as an investment.** It will pay for itself many times over in the course of your lifetime. Both men and women benefit from postsecondary education. You can earn up to $2.1 million dollars more over your lifetime by obtaining a bachelor's degree. However, the return is not the same if you do not complete your degree—so don't quit!

15. **Think about what you can do now to prepare.** If you have a job, start putting away some money from each paycheck for college.

16. **Do not allow the cost of college to spoil your education plans.** Financial aid and other money may be available from a variety of sources.

17. **Start your search up close and personal.** The most likely source of scholarships for most students is geographically close to home, and the best single identifying source of these local opportunities resides in the high school guidance office.

18. **Public libraries have resource books to help you research scholarships.**

19. **Early is essential.** Start looking at the beginning of your junior year in high school. Begin the financial aid investigation process at the same time you begin the college selection process.

20. **Be sure to confirm with your high school counselor that you have completed appropriate applications in your junior year to qualify for aid after your senior year.** For example, to qualify for the National Merit Scholarship program you must have completed the PSAT exams in the junior year of high school. Many states have scholarship programs for distinguished high school scholars, but the letters of recommendation must be received by the state scholarship administration while the student is a junior in high school.

21. **Become informed by talking with your counselor about the advantages of taking tests or classes while in high school for college credit.** This will help you save money later.

22. **The College-Level Examination Program (CLEP) allows students to demonstrate their proficiency at the college level.** By doing so, it allows the college to exempt the student from college courses (save money), lets students advance to higher level courses to complete the college requirements earlier (save more money), and exempts students from taking prerequisites or introductory courses (save even more money).

23. **The Advanced Placement (AP) program allows students to experience college-level work while still in high school.** Many colleges give credit or advanced placement to students who receive "qualifying grades" on AP exams.

24. **Marketing yourself is probably the most important aspect of receiving a merit award.** Too many students depend on grades alone to get merit scholarships for school. As many schools are looking beyond test scores for admission, the same is true for merit awards. A student who has excelled in school and contributed to other areas of interest is more likely to receive these types of scholarships. Schools are looking for students who have challenged themselves academically while still maintaining a separate life of volunteering, publishing, or conducting research.

25. **Promote yourself.** Many local scholarship donors ask that high schools do their selections. This is the focal point of your self-promotional and search activities.

26. **Don't wait for financial aid to award your job.** Apply for part-time work at a local campus while you're still in high school, even if you don't plan to attend there. College departments prefer to hire experienced employees just as other employers do. Need-based, financial aid–awarded jobs are often a small proportion of campus jobs.

27. **Make a folder for each school as you narrow down your choices.** In that folder keep information about cost, type of aid offered, deadlines, and any special scholarships the school offers. You can get the base information from brochures or from the school's Web site.

28. **Examine the free scholarship automated services that are available on most university Web sites.**

29. **Ask to talk with someone in financial aid when you visit campuses.** Admission officers know the basics of financial aid, but you want to get more detail than that. If you can't visit in person, call and ask for a phone appointment. If possible, get a name from the school's Web site and ask to talk with that particular person. Financial aid titles vary, but a "counselor" or "assistant/associate director" or "officer" will most likely be a person who actually evaluates applications for aid. Keep a record of who you talked to at each school; ask for their name, or better yet, their business card.

30. **Ask your questions directly and consistently.** Do not get caught up in the financial aid jargon.

31. **Find out whether your application/need for aid affects the probability that you will be admitted.** If so, how?

32. **Find out if the college offers merit aid.** If so, how many merit scholarships does it give? How are they determined, and who determines the recipients?

33. **If you are thinking of applying for Early Decision/ Early Action, ask if the aid policies/opportunities would be different.** Some institutions do not offer merit awards or better need-based packages to early applicants. (Note: This is primarily a private college process.)

34. **Ask how $3,000 in outside aid would change your aid package.** You can use any amount when you ask this question, but use the same amount at each school. That way you will get consistent answers about how outside aid might affect your package.

35. **Read everything you receive from the university.** Failure to read or understand due dates, penalties, and institutional policies will not relieve you of the obligations relating to this information.

36. **Study the administrative guides, catalogs, and class schedules.** Students who understand how their college operates will have a competitive advantage in every area, from financial aid to course selection. Take advantage of every technological shortcut possible, from electronic deposit of financial aid to early Web registration for classes.

37. **Talk to sophomores in college.** They will know how best to take advantage of administrative rules and exceptions, from possible early disbursements for study abroad to early registration for working students.

THE APPLICATION PROCESS

38. **Do not get intimidated by financial aid forms.** If you need help, please see your counselor. If your counselor cannot help you, they can refer you to someone who can.

39. **If your child has not yet been admitted, you should apply for financial assistance as soon as you have all the necessary income documents for the calendar year prior to the fall in which your child will start school.** For example, if your child is starting college in August or September 2003, in January or February of 2003 you should have all your financial income information from 2002 in order and apply for need-based financial aid assistance as early as possible. You can do this even if your child has not yet applied for admission to a particular college.

40. **Pay attention to deadlines.** All schools have grant aid available to those students who qualify, but many have limited funds. Students who pay attention to deadlines have an advantage over those who don't. Even if you have to estimate your figures on your FAFSA or institutional applications, you should do so. The sooner you file your application, the better your chances of receiving aid. Also, you should file your income taxes as early in the year as possible.

41. **Establish your filing date, and if necessary, make corrections later.** A needy student can lose thousands in grants each year by applying after the published priority date.

42. **Financial aid is an annual event.** You must reapply every year.

43. **Complete a FAFSA.** For those who have never applied for aid before, the primary methodology used to apply for financial aid assistance is the Free Application for Federal Student Aid, commonly referred to as the FAFSA. This document can be filled out on line at www.fafsa.ed.gov or with a paper document. The application process is free, and the information can be made available to all colleges and universities that your child is interested in attending. The FAFSA is the primary

document for establishing eligibility for need-based federal financial aid, and frequently it is used for state financial aid and institutional scholarships as well.

44. **The FAFSA must be submitted each year after January 1.**

45. **Students and parents should register with the U.S. Department of Education for the purpose of securing PIN numbers.** This will allow you to sign the FAFSA on line. Such action will speed up the processing of the FAFSA. Go to www.fafsa.ed.gov.

46. **If you are also applying for a bank loan, know your expected college graduation date.** Expected date of graduation refers to the date you expect to graduate from college (not high school). For example, most freshmen entering a bachelor's degree program in the fall of 2003 should expect to graduate in 2007. Why do lenders want to know this date? Many loans (federal and alternative) are deferred (payments don't have to be made) while the student is in school. Lenders use the expected date of graduation to put borrowers into this deferred status. So if you use your high school graduation date instead of your expected graduation date, you may be asked to start repaying your loan immediately.

47. **For bank loans, calculate what your total loan cost will be.** There are many online calculators that can tell you not only what your payment will be, but also how much you will pay in interest over the life of the loan. (See www.petersons.com)

48. **Borrow through the same lender each year.** By doing so, you avoid having to make payments to multiple agencies once you begin repayment. It also helps simplify the management of your loans.

49. **When borrowing through a bank, do not be afraid to call the lender no matter what the circumstances.** They want you to be successful in managing and repaying your student loans, so it is in their interest to hear from you.

50. **The normal expectation of the needs analysis process is that parents have primary financial responsibility in assisting their children paying for college.** Even if you feel that your financial obligation to your children ends when they go to college, becoming an independent student directly from high school is almost impossible. Only a very tightly defined group of individuals, such as orphans or students who are parents themselves and are providing support for their own offspring, qualify as independent students.

51. **Always tell the college financial aid office about any awards.** If your child has been given a scholarship by a local community organization, her eligibility for aid will probably be affected. In most cases all forms of resources available to the student, whether they are coming from the parents or from a scholarship that a student has secured from an outside agency, will be taken under consideration in any need-based financial aid award. Request that, if a reduction in aid is required, it be taken from loan awards.

52. **Re-Apply! Just because the student does not qualify for aid one year does not mean they will never qualify.** Student and family situations change, which could change eligibility status.

53. **If you were denied assistance when your first child started attending college, there are two very important reasons to reapply for financial aid assistance for your second attendee.** First, the results of the need analysis calculations are substantially different when you have two or more children in college compared to only one child in college. Second, regulations change on a frequent basis, and you may have established eligibility for new or changed financial aid programs.

54. **Complete your aid application materials completely.** Blanks make financial aid officers crazy; if the answer is zero, use 0, don't leave it blank.

55. **Parents, when you are completing the financial aid forms, remember to fill out your "student's" name, your "student's" birth date, and your "student's" Social Security number in the spaces provided, not yours.**

56. **Use completed federal income tax returns when completing the FAFSA when possible.** However, if tax returns are not available prior to meeting deadlines for your state or institution, estimate your income and complete the form. You can make changes to the application information later, but you cannot change the application date if you file late.

57. **Keep copies of everything you use to complete forms when you apply for aid.** Your school may ask for documentation to support the data you supply.

58. **Be on time.** Refer to the deadline materials you have compiled to be sure you are meeting the right deadline for each school to which you are applying. Make a checklist, record when you sent materials, and keep copies of everything. Do as much on line as possible. If you have questions about what is required or if something has been received, ask, don't assume.

59. **When mailing items that have a deadline, request a Certificate of Mailing from the post office.** This receipt will usually be honored by the institution should your materials be delayed or lost in the mail.

60. **Be Proactive! Contact the financial aid office at your selected college to make sure your file is complete and no documents are missing.** Check and double-check on a regular basis.

61. **If you have special circumstances you want the aid office to know about, send them a letter apart from your application.** Financial aid is about numbers, so if there are extra expenses you want to have considered, be sure to give the figures-less words, more figures is good!

62. **Always let your financial aid counselor know of any unusual circumstances and/or expenses.** Examples include: extraordinary medical expenses; expenses to care for the elderly, the handicapped, or people with special needs; child-care expenses (some institutions consider private education expenses, especially for areas of low performing public schools); bankruptcies and back taxes; large one-time payments; lay-offs, retirements, and resignations; and cost of attendance adjustments for travel, books and supplies, or living expenses.

DECISION TIME—EVALUATING FINANCIAL AID AWARDS

63. **Know the difference between NEED-based aid and MERIT-based aid.** Need-based aid is based on the financial need of the family. Merit-based aid is based on the student's grades and test scores.

64. **Use the financial aid information to evaluate the colleges to which you want to apply— but do not use it to exclude a college you really want to attend.**

65. **Have a "financial" safety school.** This is one you can afford no matter what. Having a financial safety school frees you up to apply to schools that may seem to be out of range financially.

66. **Know how colleges award funds.** Many out-of-state public colleges will only award out-of-state students with loans and work programs, no matter how large the unmet need gap. In contrast, most private colleges meet full need and do not gap. Therefore, when wishing to attend out-of-state colleges, in the majority of cases it may be cheaper to attend a high-cost private versus a low-cost public.

67. **If you need to borrow, remember the terms and conditions of educational loans can vary.** Make sure you understand the terms and the costs (i.e., interest rate, loan fees, and repayment schedule) of each loan you are offered.

68. **There are a variety of loans that may be awarded as part of a financial aid package.** In some cases, interest accrues while the student is attending school. If interest is accruing, consider paying the interest "as you go" to reduce your payments when your loan goes into repayment.

69. **The first time a student accepts a loan as part of a financial aid package, there are additional requirements to be met.** A student must participate in "first-time borrower" loan counseling either in person or on the Web, depending on the institution. The student must also sign a promissory note. Failure to attend to these details will delay the disbursement of the loan.

70. **Bank loans and federal Direct loans (as part of a financial aid package) include an origination fee of 3 percent.** Therefore, if your loan award is $1,000, you will actually receive $970. The origination fee is charged each time you receive one of these loans. When you repay the loan, you will repay the gross amount, in this case, $1,000. This is important when estimating the monies needed for college. Note: Some lenders may not "charge" any origination fee.

71. **Make a chart with each school's billed fees (tuition, fees, room and board).** Add your estimated travel cost and then subtract any gift aid and student loans offered to come up with what you will actually have to pay to the college. Compare these bottom line figures to determine which award is the most attractive. Beware: Some schools will put parent loans in an aid award—don't count these as "aid" at this point. Also, don't count any work-study since these funds are normally paid directly to the student as they are earned.

72. **Compare the different packaging philosophies and awarding criteria at each school you are considering.** If your child has been accepted at many highly selective institutions and has received numerous different financial aid packages and you are trying to decide which one to attend, compare the packaging philosophies. When you do this, one effective methodology is to calculate what the out-of-pocket

costs will be, how much of the award package will be in grants or scholarships versus loans, and particularly what is the expected renewability of scholarships and grants. Understanding the differences in costs and the renewability of scholarships and grants will give you a true picture of the comparative value of each of the awards. Finally, you must balance the value of the award package with the education your child will receive.

73. **There is an abundance of loans available to assist families in their quest for higher education.** All institutions have federal loan programs available to both students and parents, but in addition to the federal loans, there may be institutional or alternative private loans available. Often universities have unadvertised loans for the neediest students or for emergencies. You should request in depth information regarding loans from your counselor. Most loans may be deferred until the student is no longer enrolled at least half-time. Counselors often recommend student loans over parent loans due to the repayment options and interest rates.

74. **If there is a large discrepancy in offers among your selected schools, go back to the information you collected about each school; perhaps one award is merit and one is based on need.**

APPEALING A FINANCIAL AID AWARD

75. **If you feel that an aid award is not sufficient, you should contact the aid office immediately to discuss your concerns and ask for "reconsideration."** Start with the aid office at the school you most want to attend—if you can work things out with them, you will be set. If not, go to your second choice and so on. Do not try to get into a bidding war—these are rarely productive.

76. **Always try first to contact the Financial Aid Office directly, not the Admission Office, not an alumna, and not the president of the school!** If you have trouble

getting through, keep trying—it's a busy time. But if you can't get in touch within a week, talk to the Admission Office and see if they can help facilitate contact.

77. **Another reason for filing an appeal is that some private colleges have an appeal policy that they will meet or match any award offer from a similar college.**

78. **Have copies of all your documents on hand when you do talk with the aid officer.** If you have updated information, such as a more recent tax return, have that available as well.

79. **If you have lost your job since you completed the needs analysis document and wish to inquire about additional aid, inform the college or university that your child is planning to attend about your economic situation.** You can expect that the institution will require documentation verifying your current income. Most institutions have standard policies in place that allow for the use of projected income. Hopefully, this will increase your financial assistance.

80. **If you have substantial credit card debt, the needs analysis process does not give consideration to credit card debt in the typical calculations.** Your best course of action is to complete the FAFSA and then establish a relationship with the university's financial aid office and explain your situation. Different institutions have different policies on how they will respond to these situations.

81. **You should include information about "better" awards. But first be sure they are in fact better and also comparative.** Don't send a merit award to a school that only does need-based aid.

82. **Don't expect an answer on the spot, but do ask when you might expect a decision and how that decision will be communicated.** Assuming you contact the office in a timely manner, you should expect an answer to an aid appeal prior to the school's reply date. If you don't get one by then, ask for an extension to the reply date.

83. **Be prepared to also talk about financing options.** But only discuss this after you have determined that there is no more grant aid available.

84. **Approach an appeal as a fact-finding exercise, not a negotiation.** Always consider the person you are talking to. Aid officers have families and kids in college, bills to pay, and choices to make. They may not respond well if you insist that your vacation home is a necessity! They value you and will work hard to help you come to their school. However, ultimately they are constrained by federal and institutional policy just as you may be constrained by what your family is willing to pay. If you can't come to an arrangement that works for you, then you need to move on to your next choice of school.

CASH FLOW AND SAVINGS

85. **Campus work is available.** Most colleges employ significant numbers of their own students. They understand that college students are motivated, reliable, and smart employees.

86. **Remuneration for on-campus work is priceless, especially for new students.** Invaluable campus contacts, mentoring, and organizational smarts all become benefits to the real insider, the employee.

87. **Make sure you arrive on campus with "financial instruments" that allow you to take advantage of bargains and early decisions.** Local checking accounts, electronic transfers from financial aid, and credit cards can make early discounts available to you.

88. **Many apartment owners and landlords will discount if paid in advance for a full semester.**

89. **Buy books early, buy from other students directly, and check local bookstores.** Many books can be borrowed from local libraries and kept for entire semesters.

90. **Ask if your university provides rental of textbooks rather than purchase.** Rental is generally less expensive than outright purchase. If you purchase textbooks, be aware of the refund policy. Usually there is a date after which you cannot return a book for a refund. Is there a sliding scale for refunds on returned books? The earlier you return a book, the greater your chance of a refund.

91. **Will the bookstore buy your books back at the end of the semester?** How are returned books valued? Is the condition of the book considered? Asking these questions could maximize the refunds or resale monies for which you are eligible.

92. **Be cautious about the use of credit cards.** It's the most common way that college students create a poor credit history. It only takes one 90-day delinquency to mar your credit report. These items stay on your report for years and can prevent you from being able to get other types of credit in the future, such as auto loans, alternative loans for education, and mortgages. Credit checks are often run prior to getting an apartment, and some employers require a credit check before they will hire you. Many lenders would rather lend to someone with no credit than to someone with bad credit.

93. **Know tuition due dates and the penalties for not paying by those dates.** Many institutions charge late fees for payments after a certain date or registration after a certain date. Paying on time and registering on time can save you money.

94. **If paying tuition by credit card, be aware of any additional costs charged by the university or a third-party servicer to cover the costs they incur for accepting credit cards.** The fee may range from 1 to 3 percent of the amount charged and is in addition to the interest charge on your credit card bill.

95. **If paying tuition with a credit card in order to receive "frequent flyer miles," compare the interest you will**

pay for charging the tuition versus the value of the free miles. If you decide to charge $5,000 of tuition and pay it off in one year at an interest rate of 1.25 percent per month, you will spend approximately $406 in interest. Are the "frequent flyer miles" worth $406?

96. **Read and understand any contract you sign for campus housing.** Are there penalties if you change your mind concerning where you want to live? Do you have to maintain a certain credit load to be eligible for campus housing? Are you allowed to change rooms without financial penalty?

97. **A portion of tuition costs may qualify as a tax credit for parents and/or students contingent upon income and the method of payment.** The Hope Scholarship Credit allows deductions on a per-student basis for the freshman and sophomore years of postsecondary education, while the Lifetime Learning Credit is used on a tax-return basis and covers a more expansive timeframe and array of educational courses. Tax-free grants, scholarships, and employer-education assistance used to meet educational expenses are not eligible for either tax credit. Education expenses paid for with loans are eligible. If you want to take advantage of either of these credits, contact your tax preparer.

98. **Be aware of financial aid penalties for withdrawing from classes.** These are in addition to tuition penalties. If a student who received Title IV (federal) financial aid withdraws from all classes before the 60 percent point in the semester, the student may be required to repay some or all Title IV financial aid. This is dictated by a federal formula. Check with a financial aid counselor before withdrawing from classes and ask specifically about Title IV.

THINGS TO CONSIDER

99. **Avoid offers of guaranteed monies that you have to pay for.** Never pay for any service that you can discover on your own for free.

100. **"Free" financial aid seminars are not always free.** These invitations often come from promoters seeking unreasonable fees to provide consulting advice.

101. **Federal regulations protect the privacy of the student.** If a parent or guardian needs financial information regarding a student (i.e., balance of a student's account, payments made, etc.), check with the institution concerning its policy on student privacy. At some schools, students may stipulate that another person may have access to their financial information. Knowing the policy in advance will facilitate making payments and receiving needed information.

Special thanks to the following people for their assistance in creating this list of tips:

Dr. Lawrence Burt, Director, Student Financial Services, University of Texas Austin

Dr. Herm Davis, Executive Director of the National College Scholarship Foundation

Brenda Dillon, Vice President Federal Program Product Manager, Key Education Resources

Heather Domeier, Assistant Director of Student Financial Services, Rice University

Audrey Hill, Guidance Counselor, Zadock Macgruder High School, Rockville, Maryland

John Nametz, Director of Need Based Aid, University of Arizona

Steve Rouff, Associate Director of Financial Aid (retired), Rutgers University

Myra Baas Smith, University Director of Financial Aid, Yale University

Dr. Lawrence Waters, Dean of Admissions and Enrollment Services, Ball State University

Kathy Wyler, Bursar, University of Wisconsin-Parkside

6 Chapter

Getting Your Share of the Money

Applying for student financial aid can be complicated. This chapter gives further details about the application process for financial aid and also gives suggestions for maneuvering through some of the more troublesome areas in order to make the process simpler.

The process of applying for financial aid can be quite lengthy, and some funds, particularly grant funds, are limited. Submit all required application and follow-up forms according to the schools' deadline to ensure being considered for all available funds and to receive timely notification of the funds being offered.

Never wait until an admission offer has been made before applying for financial aid. Waiting is the surest way to miss out on the best financial aid package!

THE FREE APPLICATION FOR FEDERAL STUDENT AID (FAFSA)

As you now know, the application form that all students must use to apply for federal financial aid is called the Free Application for Federal Student Aid (FAFSA). The income, asset, and demographic information you provide on the FAFSA serves as the basis for determining your child's eligibility for the federal student aid programs and, in many cases, institutional, state, and private sources of aid.

You need complete only one FAFSA, even if your child is applying for admission to more than one school. Keep in mind that you can use the FAFSA to request that application information be sent to as many as six different schools at a time. To designate where information should be sent, the school's complete name, address, and appropriate federal school code must be provided on the FAFSA. A list of federal school codes can be found at www.ed.gov/offices/OSFAP/Students/.

First-time federal financial aid applicants must complete the regular FAFSA, which is a six-page form that contains numerous questions. Regular FAFSAs are available at most public libraries, college financial aid offices, or can be downloaded from the Internet at www.ed.gov/offices/OSFAP/Students/ apply.html. Renewal FAFSAs are mailed automatically to students who successfully complete a FAFSA the year before and are preprinted with information from your previous year's FAFSA. Simply update this information for the new school year, if necessary. Be sure to check with your financial aid administrator or call 800-4-FEDAID if you do not receive the renewal FAFSA.

Electronic Applications

The FAFSA and Renewal FAFSA also are available in electronic application formats. Some schools can electronically transmit FAFSA information directly to the Central Processsing System (CPS). Most schools now participate in the Department of Education's Electronic Data Exchange (EDE). Through EDE, a school can enter FAFSA information and transmit it directly to the CPS. Check with the financial aid offices at the schools to which your child is applying to see if any of them can electronically transmit your FAFSA data for you.

You can also apply electronically for federal student aid by using FAFSA on the Web or FAFSA Express. FAFSA on the Web is an Internet application developed by the Department of Education that can be used to complete an electronic FAFSA. Use a browser that has been certified for use with FAFSA on the Web so you don't encounter problems while entering your application that Customer Service can't resolve. By using an approved browser, you can complete and submit your FAFSA information directly to the CPS. After transmitting an application over the Internet, you can either mail your completed signature page to the FAFSA processor to complete the application process or you can electronically sign it by using a Personal Identification Number (PIN) obtained from the Web site. Once the signature page is received, the CPS prints and mails a Student Aid Report (SAR) to you. The address for FAFSA on the Web is www.fafsa.ed.gov.

FAFSA Express is a stand-alone software application tool that allows you to apply directly, in an electronic format, to the Department of Education. The software for FAFSA Express can be loaded and used from any Windows PC with direct access to a modem. The screens in the software resemble a paper FAFSA and include online help and instructions. Individual copies of the FAFSA Express software can also be obtained from colleges and universities for use on your own personal computer, or you can download FAFSA Express from the World Wide Web at www.ed.gov/offices/OSFAP/ students/apply.fexpress.html.

Visit www.fafsa.ed.gov/ beforebrowser_req.htm for the most current list of acceptable browsers. To increase the security of the application data, the Department of Education recommends that you use the "domestic version" (56-bit and 128-bit encryption) of the browser.

Supplemental Forms

Many colleges and universities may also require you to complete one or more supplemental applications, such as the College Scholarship Service (CSS) PROFILE. Note that some supplemental applications may charge a fee. These forms collect information in addition to that on the FAFSA; schools use this information to award institutional financial aid. To ensure consideration for all types of aid awarded by a school, complete all required applications. In addition, submit all required forms by the schools' published priority filing dates. As previously stated, failing to submit a form by its deadline may jeopardize your chances of receiving all of the financial assistance for which your child is eligible.

Some states also require additional information. Since required forms can vary significantly from campus to campus and from state to state, work closely with the financial aid office at each school to which you are applying. This will ensure that you have filed all of the necessary forms for all the types of aid that is available. Reviewing college catalogs, Web sites, or comprehensive college guides, such as those published by Peterson's, can also be helpful in determining whether the FAFSA is sufficient or additional applications are required.

COMPLETING THE FAFSA

In their rush to complete the FAFSA, families often make costly errors. Here are three of the biggest errors and ways to prevent them:

1. **Filling out the FAFSA incompletely or inaccurately.** Incomplete or inaccurate information can cause delays in processing applications. Errors can also result in a reduction of the total aid offered to your child.

2. **Not submitting all of the required applications for all possible sources of aid.** For example, many schools require a supplemental application for institutional aid. Confirm, and reconfirm if necessary, that you have submitted all required forms and that the appropriate individual or organization has received the form.

3. **Not submitting application forms by the published priority filing dates.** Most schools require you to submit the FAFSA and other financial aid application documents by a priority filing date. Families that miss this date are frequently offered less financial aid or less desirable financial aid than they would have been offered otherwise.

It is important to understand that when applying for financial aid you accept certain responsibilities. These responsibilities include providing correct, accurate, and timely information; reviewing and understanding the agreements contained on any of the forms you sign; complying with application deadlines and requests for additional information; and repaying any funds received as a result of inaccurate information.

Another responsibility is to check on the status of your application. If you applied on line, you should check one week after submitting the application. If you mailed in your application, or filed electronically and mailed in a signature page, check 2-3 weeks after submitting the application.

You can check the status of your application by either calling 800-4-FEDAID (toll-free) or via the Web at www.fafsa.ed.gov. Note that you can check the status via the Web site even if you mailed in your application. Anyone who checks their status on line must have a Personal

Identification Number (PIN). You can register for a PIN on the FAFSA site by clicking on "PIN site," or you can go directly to the PIN site at www.pin.ed.gov. It can take up to 5 days to receive a PIN via e-mail.

Where Application Summary Information Is Sent

When the FAFSA processor receives your completed paper FAFSA, your data is entered into a computer system and electronically transmitted to the Central Processing System (CPS). The CPS analyzes it and transmits the results of the application to you, the school, and to the state financial aid agency.

The CPS produces and sends out either a Student Aid Report (SAR) or an SAR Information Acknowledgment form. If you applied electronically through a school, you receive a one-page SAR Information Acknowledgment form; if you applied using FAFSA on the Web or FAFSA Express or completed a paper FAFSA, you receive a two-part SAR. Both the SAR and SAR Information Acknowledgment summarize information reported on your FAFSA and display your Expected Family Contribution (EFC), which we will discuss in further detail later in this chapter. When you receive either of these types of SARs, review the reported information to confirm that it is accurate.

Most schools now participate in the Department of Education's Electronic Data Exchange and receive your FAFSA information electronically so you may not need to send them a copy of the SAR. Be sure to keep a copy of the SAR for your records. If the school does ask for a copy, send the most updated version.

At the same time that the SAR is sent to you, the CPS also electronically transmits an applicant's data and an analysis to the school(s) you listed on the FAFSA. The electronic

The FAFSA is often completed before your tax forms have been filed, so the information you reported may have been estimated. If you now have more accurate information or discover that an error was made, update or correct the information. This can be done either by noting the changes on the SAR, signing it, and returning it to the FAFSA processor (or the school if it is equipped to electronically transmit these changes for students) or, if your FAFSA information was transmitted through a school using EDE, by notifying the school directly of any corrections.

information the school receives is called an Institutional Student Information Record (ISIR). Schools use this information, usually in conjunction with other documents submitted, to determine eligibility for federal, institutional, and state aid. FAFSA information is also transmitted by the CPS to your state agency so that your child may be considered for any state-sponsored financial aid programs.

Additional Document Requirements

When the school receives your output from the CPS, the financial aid office evaluates the information to determine whether additional documents are required. The documents required by each school differ somewhat depending on the types of aid the institution has to offer and whether or not you have been selected for a process called verification.

Schools usually assign a deadline for receipt of these additional documents. To avoid jeopardizing the application process, always submit required documents to the institution by those established deadlines. As stated earlier, it is important to submit documents that are complete, signed, and dated so there are no delays in processing or award notification since this can mean significant decreases in aid offered.

DEADLINES

Since deadlines are so critical to the successful completion of the application process, they are discussed once again, this time by category.

Free Application for Federal Student Aid (FAFSA)

Although the FAFSA indicates a deadline of June 30, schools usually set much earlier deadlines by which you must submit the FAFSA. These deadlines are typically in the early spring preceding the school year for which you are seeking aid: for example, by February, March, or April for the school year beginning in the fall.

Tax Returns and Institutional Applications

Frequently, schools require tax returns and institutional applications. Deadlines for these documents are usually somewhat later than the application deadline for filing the FAFSA.

Federal Programs

Some federal programs, such as Federal Pell Grants and the FFEL and Direct Loan Programs, are not dependent upon the availability of funds at a particular school. Funds for these programs are always available, provided that you can demonstrate eligibility. This is not the case with the federal campus-based programs (FSEOG, FWS, and Federal Perkins) or institutional aid for which funding is quite limited.

HOW "THEY" DECIDE WHAT YOU PAY

At this point, it is important to make a distinction between need and need analysis. Need has already been defined as the difference between your cost of attendance and your Expected Family Contribution (EFC). Your need, as determined by the school, represents the amount of money needed for your child to attend a particular school. Need analysis, on the other hand, focuses on determining the amount you can reasonably be expected to contribute toward your child's educational expenses for a given year.

Principles of Need Analysis

Since the amount of money available through the federal student aid programs is limited, the process of distributing student aid funds must be done in a fair and equal manner. To understand how need analysis works, it is important to note the basic underlying principles of the concept. These are:

> **Nobody likes deadlines and very few financial aid administrators find pleasure in denying a family financial assistance because they failed to meet one. Deadlines are used because funds are limited and for lack of a better way to ration precious resources, schools have resorted to imposing deadlines on finacial aid applicants. To ensure the best possible financial aid award, you must meet deadlines. Don't procrastinate—it can cost your child a college education.**

$ Students have a responsibility to pay for their educational costs to the extent that they are able.

$ Each student's current financial situation should be taken into consideration when determining need.

$ Need analysis must evaluate all student applicants in an equal, fair, and consistent manner.

In general, the need analysis formula considers several factors when determining how much you can reasonably be expected to contribute toward educational expenses. The two most influential factors are:

There is one methodology for determining an EFC for all federal student aid programs. Because the specifics of the formula used to assess your ability to contribute toward educational expenses were developed by the U.S. Congress and then defined by Congress in statute, the formula is appropriately named the Federal Methodology, or FM.

1. Your income

2. Your asset equity

There are other elements that can affect your ability to pay. These can include:

$ The number of people in your family

$ Family members supported on a fixed income (this means less discretionary income for college expenses)

$ The number of siblings attending college (when more than one family member is attending college, the EFC needs to be divided among several individuals instead of just one)

Overview of the Federal Methodology

The Federal Methodology (FM) is the system used to determine the EFC for the Federal Pell Grant program, the campus-based programs, and the Federal Subsidized Stafford and Direct Subsidized Loan programs. The EFC is not used to determine eligibility for Federal Unsubsidized Stafford and Direct Unsubsidized Loans. Instead, a variation of the need formula is used.

While there is only one Federal Methodology, there are three computational models contained within the methodology: the regular, simplified, and automatically assessed formulas.

The Regular Formula

The regular need analysis formula is used for most students. It evaluates your asset situation and determines a contribution from assets, an amount that is combined with available income to give an accurate picture of your financial strength. Here's how it works:

$ First, your net worth is calculated by adding assets reported on the FAFSA (negative amounts are converted to zero for this calculation). The net worth of a business/farm is adjusted to protect a portion of the net worth of these assets.

$ Second, your discretionary net worth is calculated by subtracting an education savings and asset protection allowance from your net worth. This is done to protect a portion of assets (net worth). Discretionary net worth may be less than zero.

$ Finally, the discretionary net worth is multiplied by the conversion rate of 12 percent to obtain your contribution from assets, which represents the portion of the value of your assets that may be considered to be available to help pay your child's college costs. If the contribution from assets is less than zero, it is set to zero.

Your contribution from assets is added to your available income, and this value is referred to as the adjusted available income. The adjusted available income is multiplied by an assessment rate, which is a percentage that increases as the adjusted available income increases. This finally brings us to the amount in a given year that you are expected to contribute to your child's educational expenses. If more than one household member attends college at least half-time during the same year, your EFC is divided equally among them. For instance, if your EFC were calculated to be $5,000 and your son and daughter were planning to attend college in the same year, this amount would be shared between the two children. In other words, your family would be expected to provide $2,500 for your son and $2,500 for your daughter.

Simplified Formula or Simplified Needs Test

In some very specific situations, the regular need analysis formula ignores your asset information. An EFC is computed using only your income; no contribution from assets is assessed. This formula is called the simplified needs test. A dependent student qualifies for the simplified formula if all of the following criteria are true:

$ the student's parents filed or are eligible to file an IRS form 1040A or 1040EZ, or if they are not required to file any income tax return; and

$ the student filed or is eligible to file an IRS form 1040A or 1040EZ, or if he/she is not required to file any income tax return; and

$ the income of the parents from the two sources below is $49,999 or less (excluding the student's income):

$ for tax filers, the parents' adjusted gross income from Form 1040A or 1040EZ is $49,999 or less, and

$ for non-tax filers, the income shown on the W-2 forms of both parents (plus any other earnings from work not included on the W-2s) is $49,999 or less.

It is important to emphasize that the key to qualifying for the simplified need formula is not whether you filed a 1040A or 1040EZ but rather whether you were eligible to file one of these types of tax returns. In other words, if your combined income was less than $50,000 and you filed a 1040 but were eligible to file a 1040A or 1040EZ, you would still qualify for the simplified need analysis formula.

Automatic Zero EFC

This third method of determining an EFC does not involve any calculation. Instead, you are automatically assessed an EFC of zero dollars. This model is appropriately termed the Automatic Zero EFC.

Certain students are automatically eligible for a zero EFC. For the award year, a dependent student automatically qualifies for a zero EFC if both of the following are true:

1. **the student and parents filed or are eligible to file an IRS Form 1040A or 1040EZ (they are not required to file a Form 1040), or the student and parents are not required to file any income tax return; and**

2. **the sum of both parents' adjusted gross incomes is $13,000 or less, or if the parents are not tax filers, the sum of their earned incomes is $13,000 or less.**

A Note About Special Circumstances

There may be situations in which base-year income does not provide an accurate reflection of your financial strength or other aspects of the formula that do not reasonably depict your ability to contribute to educational expenses. Under the Federal Methodology, the aid administrator may change the FM data elements in individual cases in ways that would more accurately measure your ability to pay for educational costs. These professional judgment adjustments may be made only when unusual and extenuating circumstances exist and only when you provide adequate documentation of those circumstances.

A common example of an extenuating circumstance that would lead an aid administrator to use professional judgment is when you experience a significant loss of income between the base year and the current year. This could happen as a result of a family member losing a job or having hours at work reduced. If this or a similar situation occurs, a financial aid administrator may decide to use your projected or current-year income in the need analysis formula rather than the base year, as long as you provide adequate documentation.

Chapter 7

Pulling the Pieces Together— Paying for College

Once your child's eligibility for financial aid has been established, the next step is to develop a financial aid award. The process of combining different types of aid from a variety of sources to meet your need is called packaging. It fills the gap between the cost of attending a particular school and the amount you can afford to draw from your own income and assets to pay those costs. Packaging is the way financial aid administrators seek to distribute limited resources equitably. It is important to understand that the FAFSA processor does not determine your financial need or your financial aid package. The individual schools make these decisions, and they do so by taking into account the cost of attendance, your EFC and other resources, the amount of financial aid funds available, the number of students requesting assistance, and the goals established by the school.

Timing of Packaging

Financial aid can play a very important part in your child's school selection process. Schools are aware of this and try to provide information to applicants as soon as possible so that they can make an informed choice about the school they ultimately choose to attend. Some schools even provide a preliminary aid package even before a student has been admitted; most wait until the student has been formally admitted. An offer of financial aid either accompanies the acceptance notification or follows on a separate timetable.

For schools that package based on application deadlines, there is frequently an earlier deadline for first-year students than there is for returning students. First-year applicants must be aware of the timing of admissions notifications and when they can expect to receive notification of the financial assistance. These two pieces of information are extremely important, and in many cases, the decision to attend a particular school cannot be made until you know how much financial assistance will be extended. For example, if the aid application deadline is March 15, award notifications might be sent by April 1. The school might have a reply date of May 1, by which time you must notify the school whether your child plans to attend that school (and perhaps submit a deposit to hold a place in the incoming class). Your child may have been notified of his or her acceptance for admission to the school in January but did not have a financial aid offer until April. Since you may be weighing admission offers from several schools, packaging becomes a means of tipping the scales for some schools.

A school that generally does not offer aid until a certain date or until you have completed your financial aid file may still be willing to give a preliminary estimate of the aid you are likely to receive. Therefore, if you have not yet received an offer of aid from a school in which your child is seriously interested, you should not be afraid to contact the school for information.

Before packaging can begin, the aid administrator must have the results of your FAFSA back from the CPS. It is your responsibility to ensure that the FAFSA is submitted to the FAFSA processor in time to meet school deadlines. You also must find out whether the school requires other application forms or supporting documents. It is not uncommon for schools to have their own institutional aid applications nor is it unusual for schools to require tax returns or other documents to verify or further explain data reported on the FAFSA. The federal government also requires some financial aid applicants to verify the income information reported on the FAFSA by submitting tax returns to the school's financial aid office.

It is a good idea to complete your income tax return as early as possible. This ensures that if the school or the government requires a tax return, you can promptly submit it to the school and avoid unnecessary delays in award notification.

If you were not required to file a tax return, you may be asked to provide other forms of documentation. All types of income summaries, such as W-2 forms, Social Security statements, and welfare receipts, should be kept accessible in the event they are requested by the school.

Cost of Attendance

To understand the packaging process, you must understand the concepts leading to it. We have already defined need, and we have reviewed in detail one of the components of the need equation: the EFC. The remaining component is the cost of attendance.

Cost of attendance is frequently referred to as the student budget, and it takes into consideration expenses that are related to your child's education. These educational costs include:

$ tuition and fees

$ room and board

$ books and supplies

$ transportation

$ miscellaneous personal expenses

Costs also include other types of expenses, such as loan fees, expenses related to a disability (if they are necessary for attendance and are not already covered by other assisting agencies), costs related to a study-abroad program, and costs related to a cooperative education work experience. If your child incurs other expenses during the school year that have not been mentioned, consult with your school's aid administrator as early in the aid application process as possible.

Your child is expected to live on a reasonable but modest budget while attending college. Most schools use standard budgets that reflect the average amount a student spends for each budget category. For example, rather than calculating individual budgets for each student based on their major, schools usually use an average amount for a broad category of students. Your child's actual costs may vary slightly from the standard budget, but aid is normally based on the averages. If there is some documentable reason that your son or daughter will incur costs greater than the average, be sure the aid administrator is made aware of

If your child plans on attending school less than half-time, you have a modified cost of attendance. Allowable expenses are limited to tuition and fees, books and supplies, and transportation. If your child enrolls in a correspondence program, only tuition and fees are considered. Books and supplies, travel, and room and board are included in the cost of attendance only if required for a period of residential training.

them in order to be apprised of the circumstances and to adjust the package.

The cost of attendance varies by type of institution and the costs associated with attending that institution. For example, independent (or private) colleges and universities do not receive government operational subsidies and therefore must charge students higher tuition and fees than a state-supported community college or other public institution of higher learning. Consequently, the cost of attendance at a private college or university is usually higher than that of a public college or university. The cost of attendance can also vary by individual student. A student who lives off campus may have a higher room and board cost than a student who is living in a residence hall.

Although the cost of attendance varies by institution and student, the EFC should remain relatively constant no matter which college your child decides to attend. Thus, need varies because costs vary. This is an important concept to keep in mind when helping your child decide which institution to attend.

Tuition and Fees

The tuition and fee component of your child's cost of attendance is fairly straightforward. Tuition and fees are the actual amount you are charged rather than an average based on a group of students. Depending upon the type of program your child is enrolled in, other charges such as laboratory fees and equipment costs may also be included in this category.

Room

Room includes housing costs incurred by your child. The nature of the room expense varies greatly according to the student's circumstances, depending on whether he or she lives on campus, off campus, or at home with you.

Board

Like the room expense, board is an allowance that varies according to the student's place of residence. This allowance normally provides for reasonable costs necessary to provide nutritionally adequate meals for the single student.

Transportation

For students who commute to and from campus, the transportation allowance includes the cost of getting to and from school each class day. The transportation allowance is not intended to cover the cost of purchasing a car, but it may be sufficient for parking and general maintenance of a car. The allowance is not usually adequate to pay for insurance coverage. If your child attends a school in an area where public transportation is adequate and reliable, the transportation allowance is usually based on the use of that system.

Personal Expenses

Student budgets also allow for miscellaneous personal expenses. Everyday necessities, such as personal hygiene and laundry expenses, are included in this cost category, as is a modest clothing allowance. Many schools provide a small budget for an occasional movie or other form of entertainment.

The Packaging Process

Once the school has established reasonable standard student aid budgets and the most appropriate one is selected for a particular student, the packaging process can begin. The basic principle is that the student has the first obligation to pay for educational costs.

As discussed earlier, the difference between the cost of attendance at a particular school and your ability to contribute toward those costs establishes your need for certain types of financial assistance, generally referred to as need-based aid. Again, here is the formula for need-based aid:

Cost of Attendance (COA)

– Expected Family Contribution (EFC)

= Need

If your child has been awarded some other type of assistance, such as an academic scholarship from a community organization, these resources must be taken into account when you are packaged with need-based assistance. With this in mind, here is the formula used when there are other resources to take into account:

> Cost of Attendance (COA)
>
> − Expected Family Contribution (EFC) and other resources
> _____
> = Need

The first resource considered in the packaging process is the EFC. If the EFC is equal to or greater than the cost of attendance, a school may award your child merit-based aid of its own, or you have the option of borrowing a Federal Unsubsidized Stafford Loan or Direct Unsubsidized Loan.

Before awarding any form of student assistance, the school must first determine whether you are eligible for a Federal Pell Grant. The Federal Pell Grant is considered the foundation of the aid package. All other assistance is built around this grant. The aid administrator must calculate the actual amount of the Federal Pell Grant award based upon your EFC, cost of attendance for an academic year, length of your child's period of enrollment, and his or her enrollment status.

Once eligibility for a Federal Pell Grant has been considered, the school determines whether the student will receive assistance from external sources. This type of assistance includes any state grant, private scholarships (such as service club awards and merit scholarships), and any student educational assistance benefits such as veterans' educational benefits. When all of your educational resources have been subtracted from your cost of attendance along with the EFC, any remaining need for student assistance is met with a combination of sources over which the school has control, based on the school's packaging policies and philosophy.

How Need Is Determined for Non-Need-Based Federal Programs

The amount you may receive from the non-need-based federal programs (such as Federal Unsubsidized Stafford Loan and Direct Unsubsidized

Loan) is determined somewhat differently from the other federal programs described in Chapter 3. As discussed earlier, the EFC is not considered when your eligibility for non-need-based assistance is determined. However, the amount that may be borrowed is limited to the difference between the cost of attendance at a particular institution and the estimated amount of other assistance you receive. The formula for non-need-based federal financial aid is:

Cost of Attendance

− Estimated Financial Assistance
_____

= Need

It should now be clear that the amount of aid you receive is directly related to the cost of attendance at schools. The EFC should be constant from school to school, unless your EFC is adjusted based on individual unusual circumstances by the aid administrator at one school but not at another.

If your child applies to two schools (one high-cost and the other low cost), it is quite possible that the amount of aid offered by the high-cost school will be enough to cover the difference in costs between the two. By offering more aid, the actual cost to you is the same regardless of which school the student actually attends. When this occurs, one of the fundamental purposes of student aid is accomplished: to provide access and choice. You may incur a heavier debt burden or your child may be required to work more hours at one school versus another. You may decide that it is worthwhile to assume this additional responsibility if it means your child will be able to attend the school of his or her choice. Methods for comparing aid packages will be discussed in more detail later in this chapter.

> **The Federal Unsubsidized Stafford Loan and Direct Unsubsidized Loan may be used to replace all or part of your EFC. In addition, you can also borrow from these loan programs to replace any unmet need. In the case of unsubsidized loans for which you are the borrower, you must apply for any subsidized loan eligibility first.**

Examples of Financial Aid Packages

The following sample financial aid packages illustrate how aid may be combined in different ways and in accordance with differing packaging philosophies to meet your needs. Keep in mind that these are only examples; the actual financial aid packages offered by your school will almost certainly be different. When reviewing the sample packages, it is important to note that they embody the following important points:

1. **the cost of attendance will vary significantly according to school type (e.g., public versus private, two-year versus four-year),**

2. **the amounts and sources of aid will vary by school, and**

3. **the single constant in the various aid packages is the EFC.**

Community College Aid Package (full-time, first-year student)	
Budget	$5000
Expected Family Contribution	−2000
Need	$3000
Federal Pell Grant	1175
State Grant	500
Federal Perkins Loan	500
Federal Stafford Loan	− 825
Unmet Need	$ 0

In this example, the cost of attendance at the community college is relatively low. The student's financial need is completely met through grants and loans.

Public University Aid Package (full-time, first-year student)	
Budget	$9000
Expected Family Contribution	−2000
Need	$7000
Federal Pell Grant	1175
State Grant	1000
Federal Perkins Loan	1000
Federal Work Study	800
Federal Stafford Loan	−2625
Unmet Need	$400

In this example, the cost of attending a public state school is greater than the cost of the community college, primarily because the fees are higher. Note that the Expected Family Contribution (EFC) is the same as the community college example.

Although cost is a factor in calculating Federal Pell Grants because of the way in which Pell Grant awards are determined, the student's Federal Pell Grant amount remains the same. Since tuition and fees are higher at a state university than they are at a community college, this student is eligible for a larger state grant. The state university in this example has included a Federal Stafford Loan of $2625 in the package. This was done so that more of the student's need could be met. If the student decides to accept this loan, he or she will have to complete and submit, directly to the school, a loan application for the Federal Stafford Loan. If the student declines this loan, the school may not be willing or able to replace it with another form of aid. Instead, the student will have to come up with this money on his or her own, possibly through employment or from personal savings.

Private University Aid Package (full-time, first-year student)	
Budget	$18,000
Expected Family Contribution	−2000
Need	$16,000
Federal Pell Grant	1175
State Grant	2500
Outside Scholarship	1800
Institutional Grant	5000
Federal Perkins Loan	1500
Direct Stafford Loan	2625
Federal Work-Study	−1400
Unmet Need	$0

In this example, the cost of attendance is considerably greater than in the previous two examples. Again, because the tuition and fees are higher, this student is eligible for a larger state grant than he or she would have received at either the community college or state university. The aid offered also includes a Direct Stafford Loan for $2625. The student must sign a Direct Loan promissory note to receive these funds. In addition, most private universities have their own institutionally sponsored financial aid programs. Institutional aid provides financial assistance in addition to federal and state financial aid programs. Because this student has a large amount of need, he or she has been offered an institutional grant of $5000.

CHANGES TO THE AID PACKAGE

While packaging policies affect the amounts and types of aid initially offered, they also influence the ways in which adjustments are made to your award when circumstances change. Most often, adjustments are made to an aid package because the resources available to you have changed. For instance, if your child receives additional private grant funds from an outside organization after a package has been developed and offered, the aid administrator must review that package to see if it is still valid. Since federal regulations limit the amount of aid you can receive and because institutional aid is limited, financial aid administrators are usually required to reexamine your eligibility for assistance when they become aware that additional resources are available.

The school determines the manner in which a financial aid package is adjusted. If the outside source of funding is in the form of a grant, the school's policy may be to reduce grant aid already offered to you. The school may have a policy to replace loans with outside resources in order to reduce your total debt burden. If your full need had not been previously met, the school might have a policy that allows outside resources to replace unmet need before affecting aid already offered. The need of other students and the extent of available funding for each type of aid program ultimately influence the way packages are adjusted.

You are obligated to notify schools of any additional resources you receive even after the school has extended an aid offer to you. To comply with federal requirements, schools must ensure that financial aid applicants do not receive more federal aid than permitted. If you are receiving non-need-based assistance, such as an unsubsidized Federal Stafford Loan or Direct Unsubsidized Loan or a scholarship, the total aid received cannot exceed your cost of attendance.

If the financial aid administrator becomes aware of an educational expense not already covered by the standard student budget, the cost of attendance can be increased so the additional resources pay for that expense rather than decreasing the aid offered. Similarly, the EFC may be adjusted to avoid an overaward if there are extenuating circumstances.

EVALUATING AID PACKAGES

Once your child has been admitted to a school and has received offers of financial assistance, the decision-making process begins. If your child has a strong preference for one particular school, you will probably accept any offer of aid that makes attendance at that school possible. However, your child may have more than one preference, and the choice may not

When evaluating financial aid offers from various schools, your child's educational objectives must be considered as well as financial need; to the extent possible, his or her educational aspirations should be the primary consideration when selecting a school.

be so simple. In these situations, financial aid plays an important role in the decision-making process.

Once the educational aspects of the decision-making process have been considered, other factors should become part of your evaluation of financial aid offers. First, be aware that the largest financial aid package is not always the best. Because of differences in cost of attendance between the various types of schools, the largest offer in terms of dollars can also be the one with the greatest gap between cost and available resources. If that gap cannot be filled by some other source, the largest offer may not be enough for your child to attend that school.

Even two offers that fully meet your need may not be equal. If the estimated expense budget used to calculate your need is unrealistically low, you may have more real unmet need than the award letter suggests. Compare the stated costs with those of similar schools to verify the reasonableness of a school's estimated cost of attendance figures.

Packages containing equal dollars and similar unmet need are not always the same either. You may have a higher proportion of gift aid and, consequently, a smaller loan and work obligation. Or, one package may offer a higher proportion in self-help aid and less grant aid. Similarly, not all scholarships are the same. Some are automatically renewable; others are renewable only under certain conditions, such as continued high academic performance. Some are nonrenewable and good for the first year only. So a $500 scholarship that is renewable might actually be better than a $1000 scholarship with many conditions associated with it or a $1500 nonrenewable one.

For some students, certain types of packages are better than others. If your child plans to enter a low-paying profession or faces postgraduate and professional training before entering the job market, you should look more cautiously at substantial loan obligations. Equal loan amounts do not necessarily equate to the same level of obligation. While the terms and conditions of the specific federal loan programs are the same from school to school, there are variations among the types of federal loan programs offered. Higher interest rates, fewer deferment options, earlier payback requirements, and higher minimum payments can make one loan more costly than another, even when the same amount is borrowed.

When evaluating loans, it is helpful to understand the terms and conditions of each program. While Federal Perkins, Federal Stafford, and Direct Loan Programs have relatively low interest rates, the Federal Perkins Loan has different deferments and more cancellation provisions than the Federal Stafford and Direct Loans. Remember, since they can have a significant impact upon your child's postgraduate activities and the quality of his or her life after graduation, loans deserve a great deal of your attention during the evaluation process.

In assessing aid packages, bear in mind that you must repay loans regardless of whether or not your child completes his or her program of study. Dropping out of school or not being able to find a job in a chosen career does not relieve you of the obligation to repay an educational loan.

> **If you decide to borrow, make conservative but realistic estimates of the amount you actually need. The best advice is to borrow only what is needed. Also, keep track of the amounts you borrow, from whom, and when the loan or loans become payable. This is essential information for avoiding loan default. Defaulting on your education loans can have a negative effect on your credit rating and affects your ability to borrow in the future.**

AWARD NOTIFICATION: WHAT ALL THE PAPER MEANS TO YOU

There are two other important components of the financial aid process that need to be discussed: notification of the aid being offered to your child, and the delivery of that aid. To put the pieces of the financial aid puzzle together to form a complete picture, you need to know what you can expect to receive in response to your applications for aid, as well as what you must do once an offer of assistance has been extended.

Because there are many potential sources of aid, to secure funding you must usually complete and submit numerous forms and documents. Not surprisingly, you can expect to receive a great deal of paper in response. Anticipate receiving some or all of the following types of responses from application processors and schools:

$ Student Aid Report (SAR) or SAR Information Acknowledgment from the Central Processing System (CPS)

$ Notification of aid from a state agency regarding eligibility for a state scholarship, grant, or some other form of state assistance

$ Notification of aid from private sources, if applicable

$ Preliminary estimate from the school of the amounts and types of aid for which you may be eligible

$ If necessary, a letter from the school requesting additional documents, such as an institutional application, tax returns, and other documents required for verification

$ Financial aid notification (award letter) from the school

$ Loan applications or promissory notes

The Student Aid Report

In response to filing the Free Application for Federal Student Aid (FAFSA), a Student Aid Report (SAR) or a SAR Information Acknowledgment is sent from the Central Processing System (CPS). If you submitted a paper FAFSA directly to the FAFSA processor, used FAFSA Express, or used FAFSA on the Web, you will receive a SAR consisting of two parts. If you submitted a FAFSA directly to the school for electronic transmission to the CPS, you will receive a one-page, noncorrectable SAR Information Acknowledgment.

The SAR summarizes the application data you supplied on the FAFSA and provides information about the amount that you are expected to pay for your child's educational costs in the upcoming year. The SAR also provides you with instructions about what to do next. For example, if you have a problem with your Social Security Number, the SAR provides instructions about the steps that must be taken to correct the problem.

In most cases, you do not have to submit your SAR to the school your child plans to attend unless there are errors in the information reported on the SAR. It is important to understand that all schools must have an official EFC from the Central Processing System to make an award.

Schools are generally able to obtain your official EFC electronically. This electronic output document is called an Institutional Student Information Record, or ISIR.

Notification of State Aid

To be considered for a state award, some states may require you to file documents in addition to the FAFSA. The information that state agencies receive contains your financial information as well as a calculation of your EFC. In most cases, state agencies use this information to determine eligibility for state assistance; others award state aid via the school's aid administrator in compliance with state guidelines.

State aid is often channeled directly to your child's school and is always considered as an available resource when your award package is constructed. Pay particular attention to the terms and conditions of state aid, as it may be restricted to use in state, to specific components of the cost of attendance (such as tuition and fees only), or, in the case of special awards, to particular majors. If your child has been offered state assistance, he or she will have to return a signed acceptance of the state award by a specified deadline. Again, any published deadline should be taken with the utmost seriousness; failure to reply by a specified date usually results in the award being canceled, and except in extraordinary circumstances, the state aid is not reinstated.

Many states notify the school that you have been awarded state assistance. However, because this practice is not uniform, it is wise to notify your child's intended schools directly that he or she is the recipient of a state award. Schools can then take the state award into consideration when constructing your financial aid package. Otherwise, you might find out what impact the state award has on your package after your child has enrolled.

Notification of Aid from Private Sources

The award notification techniques of private aid sources vary in style and timing. In some cases, you receive some type of acknowledgment, whether or not you actually receive any money. In others, only successful applicants are contacted. Some organizations notify you in the spring that you have won an award; others notify you in the summer and sometimes not until the fall term.

Should you receive funding from a source outside of the school, it is crucial that you inform the financial aid office immediately. Failure to do so can result in your having to repay all or part of the aid received and can jeopardize future aid eligibility.

Institutional Financial Aid Award Letters

Upon receipt of all of the necessary information and forms, the financial aid administrator can finally develop a financial aid package that is designed to meet your needs. Once a package has been constructed, most schools send you a document known as an Award Letter, a Notification of Financial Assistance, or an Offer Letter. We will refer to any type of award notification as an Award Letter.

An Award Letter describes the sources, types, and amounts of financial aid being offered and is a type of commitment or contract between your child and the school. Take the terms and conditions of the award seriously and do nothing to jeopardize the assistance. This includes carefully and thoroughly reading the information enclosed with the Award Letter and responding to all required deadlines. Because financial aid resources are limited, schools often cancel awards made to students who fail to return forms on time. This aid is then reoffered to other needy and eligible students. While aid administrators work diligently to ensure that as many deserving students as possible receive assistance, they cannot extend aid offers indefinitely. You must accept the responsibility of keeping in contact with the school or risk losing the aid that has been offered to you.

Award Letters from individual schools differ in style and format, but the same basic information is generally provided. Ideally, the Award Letter, and any accompanying materials, provides specific and easy-to-understand information about:

$ Your cost of attendance

$ Your need for assistance and how that need was determined

$ A listing of the types of aid being offered to meet your need

$ When the aid will be disbursed: before, on, or after the start of classes; periodically during the term; by semester, trimester, quarter, or some other frequency, depending on the schools academic calendar

$ How it will be disbursed (by crediting your student account or by cash payment to you)

$ Any conditions of the offer, such as academic requirements, minimum course load, or satisfactory academic progress

Schools frequently require you to accept or decline the types of aid being offered and sign and return the Award Letter to the financial aid office. If a loan has been offered, you also have to sign additional forms, such as a promissory note. If an FFEL loan has been offered, you have to complete an Application and Promissory Note before any money can be disbursed.

> **You must carefully review and fully understand the types of aid being offered and the respective stipulations of the aid. Whenever you have questions or are uncertain about anything in the Award Letter, you should contact the financial aid office.**

Responding to the Award Letter

Accept, decline, or seek clarification. These are the possible responses to a financial aid Award Letter. Accepting an award is usually as simple as signing the Award Letter, although, as we mentioned earlier, additional application forms for specific funds or promissory notes for loans may be required. Declining an award is almost as important as accepting an award. Because funds are limited, schools attempt to redirect declined awards to other needy and eligible students. Most awards must be declined in writing. Usually this is as simple as marking a box on the Award Letter that states the aid is being declined, signing the letter, and returning it to the school. Keep in mind that some schools may redirect funds if you do not respond by a certain date.

You may also reject or decline certain types of aid offered. For instance, you may wish to accept a Federal Work-Study award but decline a loan. Or you may wish to accept only a portion of a specific award. For example, your child may have been offered a Federal Stafford Loan of $2625. If, after carefully reviewing your budget and resources, you determine that it's possible to get by on less, you may choose to borrow only $2000. Always consider declining a grant carefully, since a grant is money that does not have to be paid back or earned. No matter what the situation, you should respond to all aid offers made and, if possible, provide a short reason why any aid is being rejected.

When your child receives the Award Letter, you may feel that the offer is insufficient or you may wish to request a change in the types of aid that have been awarded (for example, replace a loan with work). You may want to discuss the treatment of a private scholarship or apprise the aid administrator of special family circumstances that may affect the award. Any of these situations necessitates a discussion with the financial aid administrator. If you are unhappy, unsatisfied, or simply confused about your child's aid offer, contact the school. Furthermore, if you have a delicate or complicated situation, schedule an appointment to meet with an aid administrator and, if necessary, bring any relevant information or documentation to the appointment.

Never reject a preferred school or, worse yet, decide not to proceed with your child's education on the basis of insufficient financial aid. Instead, consult with an aid administrator and discuss possible alternatives. Aid administrators work diligently to ensure that deserving students are not denied access to higher education for financial reasons. They try to be sensitive to special circumstances, but to do that, they must be aware that special circumstances exist.

FINANCIAL AID BEYOND THE FIRST YEAR

Never assume that your child will receive similar financial aid awards in subsequent years, even if he or she plans to attend the same school. Awarding policies vary from school to school, and some schools award different types of aid packages depending upon your child's grade level. Some schools award more grant aid and less self-help aid in the first year. As the student gains experience and the risk of failure diminishes, these types of schools increase the amount of loan or work offered to you in later years. Schools with discretionary institutional funds may reward high achievers with larger grant or merit-aid awards in future years. Other schools attempt to maintain the level of assistance offered to incoming first-year students throughout their school career. Don't be afraid to ask the financial aid administrator about the school's awarding policies.

HOW AND WHEN FINANCIAL AID IS PAID

Part of the award notification process includes an explanation of how and when the financial aid is paid. Financial aid can be paid using a number of different methods. A school can directly credit your child's school account with financial aid funds, it can make a cash payment to you, or it can disburse aid using a combination of these two methods. Typically, a school credits financial aid funds to your child's school account to pay for school charges such as tuition and fees. If you have remaining financial aid funds owed to you, the school pays you the balance, usually by issuing you a check. This money can be used to pay for educational expenses like books and supplies, transportation costs, off-campus room and board, and miscellaneous personal items.

Typically, the Award Letter reflects the amount of aid that can be received for the entire academic year. The aid offered, though, must be disbursed to you in increments rather than in one lump sum. If your child's school is on a quarter system, one third of your financial assistance is usually disbursed at the beginning of the fall quarter, another third at the beginning of the winter quarter, and the remaining third at the beginning of the spring quarter. If he or she is attending a school on a semester system, one half of the aid is usually disbursed at the beginning of the fall semester, and the rest at the beginning of the spring semester.

> **Most schools disburse all of your funds for a particular term at the beginning of that term. However, in an attempt to assist students in budgeting their funds, some schools make several smaller payments throughout the course of each academic term.**

WHAT IS NEXT?

Once you have accepted the school's offer of financial assistance, you also need to be aware of some issues related to the receipt of such aid.

$ The amount of grant aid your child receives in excess of the cost of tuition, fees, and course-related expenses such as books and supplies is generally considered to be taxable income and, as such, must be reported on his or her U.S. income tax return.

$ A work-study award simply means that your child is eligible to earn that amount of money during the award year. Before he or she can be paid, the student must obtain a work-study position and then work the hours necessary to earn the full amount of the award. Work-study does not mean your child will get paid for studying.

$ You may be required to submit a separate loan application to apply for and receive money from the Federal Stafford Loan Program or PLUS Loan Program. The school's financial aid office can provide you with the application materials and information about participating lenders. While other federal loan programs do not require separate loan applications, you have to sign promissory notes before any funds from these programs can be disbursed.

Chapter 8

Other Ways to Trim College Costs

When it comes to paying for school, resourcefulness is as important as resources. The shift in federal support away from grant funds created an environment where loans are the most prevalent form of financial aid. Borrowing means deferring payment for something that you want now. Simply signing on the bottom line of a loan form is the quickest and, unfortunately, easiest way to get money for education. But it can be costly, so you should look for other resources and ways to reduce costs.

The strategies that follow may not be appropriate or available to everyone, but they give you options to consider. They include:

$ Reducing your college budget

$ Earning college credit on an accelerated basis (reducing the length of time your child is in school)

$ Earning college credit outside the traditional classroom

$ Making use of payment alternatives

$ Tax credits

$ Combining higher education and course-related employment

$ National and community service

REDUCING YOUR BUDGET

Just as increasing resources is one way to meet need, so is reducing your budget.

Packaging of aid by the school is based on the school's definition of cost, which involves some assumptions and averaging. The standard nature of the budget means that it is designed for a typical student with average needs. Your child may actually spend more or less than the budget allows, but this individual variation generally does not affect the amount of aid the school offers. A standard budget assumes that you limit expenditures to reasonable levels. Your child is not expected to live below the poverty level, but he or she is expected to accept some sacrifices in order to obtain an education. To determine whether these standard costs can be reduced, you must examine them carefully and then examine your child's level of expectations about living on limited means.

Generally speaking, if your child spends more than the standard budget allows, you will have difficulty paying for school. On the other hand, if he or she is able to economize, you may end up with less debt. Or, if you repay part of your loan with money you have saved before the loan actually comes due, you can save interest charges and may be able to lower your monthly repayment.

Since a good deal of discipline is needed to resist spending money, you may prefer to accept less of a loan than could otherwise be borrowed. Before making this decision, consider the source and continuing availability of the loan. If you turn down part or all of a Federal Perkins Loan, which may offer the best deferment and cancellation provisions, the amount you decline will be offered to another needy student. If at a point later in the year you find that you really do need the Federal Perkins Loan, funds may no longer be available in that program. Then you might need to take a loan that carries less favorable terms.

The FFEL and Direct Loan Programs are not subject to the same limitations as the Federal Perkins Loan. In the case of the FFEL programs, unless the lender has a restriction on the number of applications it accepts from a student in a given year, you can borrow additional funds later as long as you show eligibility. Keep deadlines in mind since funds must normally be disbursed while your child is still enrolled. You and your child should weigh the temptation of spending any money you have, your own propensity toward saving, and the source of the loan before deciding to turn it down or to delay applying for it.

Tuition

With the exception of ruling out higher-cost schools, you cannot control the level of tuition schools charge. The amount charged for tuition varies among schools and can also vary among programs of study within a school. Cost is not always an indicator of quality or prestige, so don't rule out lower-cost schools that also offer the programs of study in which your child is interested.

Most four-year programs include a certain level of liberal arts course work required for the degree; this course work does not directly affect the major. Your child may be able to take certain preparatory courses at a lower-cost school and then transfer to a higher-cost school for more advanced courses in the program of his or her choice.

If the student intends to transfer to another school, he or she may well encounter a whole new set of deadlines and procedures. Different forms of aid might also be available, and the application process may differ significantly. Obtaining complete information well in advance of the time he or she actually transfers from one school to another is crucial for achieving a smooth transition.

Unlike private schools, public school tuition is usually affected by the state residency status of the student. Because they benefit from tax revenues, public colleges generally charge lower tuition, particularly to students who are residents of the state. Nonresident students at public schools are usually assessed a higher tuition rate. Distinguishing between resident and nonresident students at public colleges and universities appears to be a straightforward matter, but that distinction may be fairly complicated. Some states require a minimum length of residency in order to take advantage of in-state tuition. Students in the military assigned to a particular location, students who own property in another state or district, and international students who have resided in this country for a short time may discover that some schools or states will eye the bid for resident

There may be costs other than dollars that a transfer student experience, such as adjusting to a new school and its atmosphere. If your child chooses to first attend a lower-cost school to save money and then transfer to a higher-cost school, carefully consider whether all of his or her course work at the first school will be compatible with the requirements of the second school. Otherwise, you may end up losing money by having to stay in school longer or by doubling up on course work.

tuition rates with reservations. Questions on application forms about your addresses over a period of time, the state in which your child has a driver's license, and location of voter registration assist schools in determining residency status. Since the difference between resident and nonresident tuition can be hundreds or even thousands of dollars per year, seek clarification from schools under consideration.

Community College

Two-year colleges are usually funded in part by local or state taxes, so tuition is less expensive than at four-year colleges (about half the price of a public four-year college and 85 percent less than a private four-year college). A student can enroll at a community college for a year or two and take introductory and prerequisite courses at a significantly lower cost and then transfer to a four-year school to take courses in his or her major. Another way this will help you save money is room and board costs since students can live at home and commute to local community colleges. Before enrolling in community college classes, get in touch with the four-year school that your child wants to attend because not all community college courses are transferable.

SHORTENING THE PROGRAM OF STUDY

Your child may be able to earn a degree or certificate in a shorter than normal period of time. For example, he or she might consider taking one extra course per term. Over a period of time, this can easily result in early graduation. Some schools do not charge more for enrolling in additional courses over and above the school's minimum definition of full-time course load, while others charge by the credit hour. Even if there are additional charges for extra courses, ultimate savings on other expenses can be considerable.

Summer courses are another alternative. While financial aid may be available during summer school, you need to ascertain whether receiving aid during the summer reduces the amount of aid you can have for the rest of the year or program of study.

College Credit by Examination

Another approach your child can take to reduce costs is to earn credit by examination, thus reducing the amount of time required to receive a degree or certificate. Several programs that are national in scope are described in this section: AP, CLEP, PEP (Regents College in New York), and DANTES. Although you must pay an examination fee, the tests can offer cost-saving shortcuts to your child's educational destination.

Be aware that schools differ in their treatment of credits earned through examination, so find out whether the school also charges a fee for establishing the credit on your child's academic record. It is also common for schools to prescribe a minimum number of credits that must be earned on campus if a student is to receive a degree from that school. Others simply limit the number of credits that can be earned by examination. If your child transfers, you may find that the new school does not accept credits granted by a previous school if they were earned in this manner. This can be particularly true if you transfer from a two-year to a four-year college, since two-year colleges traditionally have a more liberal policy with respect to credit by examination.

Advanced Placement Program

The Advanced Placement (AP) Program offers high school students the opportunity to complete college-level studies in subjects that range from biology to Spanish to English literature. At the conclusion of the class, students take a nationally administered exam in that subject area. If the student earns a high enough score, he or she may be able to earn college credit. Some students have been known to take so many AP exams that they have skipped their freshman year of college. The monetary value of potential AP credits is easy to determine. Consider the price of a year's worth of tuition and room and board. The more expensive a university is, the more money you will save if your child can skip a year through the AP program.

Colleges and universities set their own policies on the use of AP scores to grant appropriate placement or credit for entering freshmen. A list of participating colleges is available from the College Board. However, specific questions about AP policies are best answered by officials at the college to which your child is applying for credit.

College-Level Examination Program

The College Board offers the College-Level Examination Program (CLEP). CLEP operates on the premise that college-level accomplishment can be gained not only in the classroom but also by independent study and experience. If your child has pursued hobbies, talents, or interests to a high level of proficiency, you might consider turning that pursuit into college credit through the CLEP program.

There are two types of CLEP examinations, the General Examinations and the Subject Examinations. The General Examinations measure college-level achievement in five basic areas of the liberal arts: English composition, humanities, mathematics, natural sciences, and social sciences and history. These exams test material that is usually covered in the first two years of college and that would normally be considered part of the general or liberal education requirement. The General Examinations are not intended to measure specialized knowledge of a particular discipline, nor are they based on a particular curriculum or course of study. Rather, they are designed to evaluate broad-based ability that can be acquired in a number of ways, through personal reading, employment, television, radio, adult classes, or advanced high school work.

The Subject Examinations measure achievement in specific college courses and are used to grant exemption from and credit for these courses. Twenty-nine Subject Exams are offered in subjects that range from American government to macroeconomics and from English literature to information systems and computer applications. While there are no established curricula for subjects, texts and review books have been designed to help prepare for the tests.

Excelsior College Examinations

Your child can actually obtain an associate or baccalaureate degree in certain areas of concentration through Excelsior College of the University of the State of New York (formerly known as Regents College). The program (formerly known as the Proficiency Examination Program, or PEP) combines elements of proficiency testing, correspondence courses, life experiences, military courses, and actual college instruction in measuring progress toward a degree. The program itself offers no courses but assesses college-level knowledge and evaluates the number of credits your child has accumulated by a variety of acceptable methods. A degree is awarded when requirements have been fulfilled.

Excelsior College Examinations match the subject matter taught in standard college courses and measure knowledge in specific subjects. Four general areas of testing are:

$ arts and sciences

$ nursing

$ business

$ education.

Credit can be given for introductory- through upper-level knowledge, depending on the content of the test. The tests are developed and administered by Excelsior College and are given at Prometric Testing Centers throughout the United States and Canada. Detailed study guides are provided for each test. Each guide contains a content outline, bibliography, and sample questions.

> **Credits awarded through Excelsior College may be accepted as transfer credits by approximately 1,000 colleges and universities. Many schools also use the tests to perform their own evaluation of a student's college-level knowledge and award credit. Exams are offered free to members of the U.S. military through the DANTES Examinations Program.**

Defense Activity for Non-Traditional Education Support (DANTES)

The DANTES program allows students to validate their grasp of knowledge and skills that would normally be acquired in college courses but that have instead been acquired through independent self study and on-the-job and life experiences. 1,400 colleges and universities in the United States award credit to students who receive high enough scores on more than thirty-five DANTES Subject Standardized Tests (DSST) in business, the humanities, social science, mathematics, physical science, and applied technology. The tests are administered primarily to current or previous members of the Armed Forces. Civilians may also take DSST exams, for a fee, year-round at colleges and universities throughout the United States and around the world. Before registering for an exam, check with your child's college or university to be sure that it will accept DSST credit for passing scores.

PAYMENT ALTERNATIVES

Once true costs have been ascertained and all resources have been researched and settled, options still remain to help you with your Expected Family Contribution. Most schools allow you to apply financial aid to school charges for tuition, fees, housing, meals, etc. If the aid has not actually been received, many schools allow you to defer payment until funds become available. If there is sufficient aid to cover all or most of the school's charges, the EFC is actually used for costs not directly charged by the school, such as books and supplies, transportation or commuting costs, and personal expenses. If your child commutes from home or lives off-campus, expenses not owed to the school up front would include daily meals and perhaps monthly rent or mortgage.

> **Institutional charges are very often divided among terms (such as semesters or quarters) so that the part of the EFC that does have to be used for school charges may be spread out into two or more payments rather than one. The EFC may not seem quite so overwhelming if you understand that it does not need to be furnished up front in one lump sum.**

Payment Plans

When very little or no financial aid is available, payment plans are usually available. These payment plans are either administered by the school itself or contracted to an outside agency that charges a nominal fee. Payments typically begin a few months before the start of the school year and continue for the next twelve months or more. This is basically an installment plan, usually without interest charges. Such a plan may be preferable to taking a loan and may be just enough help to avoid the necessity of an Unsubsidized Federal Stafford, Direct Unsubsidized, or PLUS Loan. For more information, contact the school's business office.

Savings Plans

An increasing number of states have sanctioned savings plans through bond sales. The savings instrument might be zero-coupon bonds or general obligation bonds. Conditions vary from state to state, so check with your state agency for more details. Under federal tax law, individuals who purchase Series EE U.S. Savings Bonds on or after January 1, 1990, can exclude from taxation all or part of the interest earned on those bonds, subject to certain limitations, if they are paying qualified educational expenses (i.e., tuition and fees for themselves, their spouse, or their dependents).

Home Equity Loan or Line of Credit

Many families pay some of their college expenses by borrowing against the equity in their home. Usually you can qualify for a home equity line of credit (which allows you to borrow when you need it, not all at once like a loan) at a rate considerably less than any other type of loan. In addition, home equity loans and lines of credit may be tax deductible, although you should always check with a tax adviser to be sure.

TAX CREDITS

Hope Scholarship

The federal government also provides certain tax credits for students who qualify. The Hope Scholarship is actually a tax credit, not a scholarship. Tax credits are subtracted from the tax you owe rather than reducing taxable income like a tax deduction. You must file a tax return and owe taxes to take advantage of it. The Hope credit is not refundable if you do not pay taxes or owe less in taxes than the maximum amount of the Hope tax credit for which you are eligible.

A family may claim a tax credit up to $1,500 per tax year per student for the first two years of undergraduate study. You can claim up to 100 percent of the first $1,000 of your eligible educational expenses and 50 percent of the next $1,000, for a maximum credit of $1,500. The actual amount of the credit depends on your income, the amount of qualified tuition and fees paid, and the amount of certain scholarships and allowances subtracted from tuition.

You are eligible for the maximum benefit with an adjusted gross income (AGI) of up to $50,000 for a single taxpayer or $100,000 for married taxpayers. The credit amount is phased out between $40,000 and $50,000 for single taxpayers and $80,000 and $100,000 for married taxpayers. Your child must be enrolled at least half-time in an eligible program leading to a degree or certificate at an eligible school during the calendar year. To claim the Hope tax credit, you must complete IRS Form 8863.

The Lifetime Learning Tax Credit

Like the Hope Scholarship, Lifetime Learning is a tax credit available to individuals who file a tax return and owe taxes. This means the amount of the credit is subtracted from your actual tax liability. The Lifetime Learning credit is not refundable.

As a taxpayer, you can claim a tax credit up to $1,000 for all students in your family per tax year, per tax return. The credit is not limited to two years of study, like the Hope, but for an unlimited number of years. You can claim up to 20 percent of the first $5,000 of eligible expenses for expenses paid after June 30, 1998, and prior to January 1, 2003, and up to 20 percent of $10,000 of eligible expenses for expenses paid after January 1, 2003.

The actual amount of the credit depends on your income, the amount of qualified tuition and fees paid, and the amount of certain scholarships and allowances subtracted from tuition. This credit is family based (e.g., $1,000 per family). To be eligible, you must file a tax return and owe taxes. You are eligible for the maximum benefit with an adjusted gross income (AGI) of up to $40,000 for a single taxpayer or $80,000 for married taxpayers. The credit amount is phased out between $40,000 and $50,000 for single taxpayers and $80,000 and $100,000 for married taxpayers. To claim the Lifetime Learning tax credit, you must complete IRS Form 8863.

NATIONAL AND COMMUNITY SERVICE (AMERICORPS)

The National and Community Service Trust Act of 1993 established the Corporation for National Service, which offers educational opportunities through service to American communities. Each state has a commission for national service through which participants are recruited and programs of service organized. The Corporation is the parent organization for the two AmeriCorps programs:

$ AmeriCorps—National Civilian and Community Corps (NCCC)

$ AmeriCorps—VISTA

The AmeriCorps Programs are designed to reward individuals who serve communities with educational benefits and to address specific needs in the areas of education, human services, public safety, and the environment.

Currently, successful completion of one year of full-time service provides an award of $4,725. If your child already has student loans, he or she may be eligible for a loan deferment. Awards may be used for past, present, or future expenses, including those for two- and four-year colleges, training programs, and graduate and professional programs. Additional information on the AmeriCorps program is available on the Internet at www.cns.gov.

> **Your child may serve before, during, or after postsecondary education. He or she must complete either one year of full-time service or two years of part-time service in an approved program in order to earn an educational award.**

MILITARY SERVICE

The military offers several ways your child can reach his or her educational goals. Military educational programs benefit men and women who serve in the country's defense forces. Participants can receive an education while serving in the military or serve in the military first and then concentrate on postsecondary education. Some programs offer only one of these options while others combine them.

Educational Benefits for Veterans

The current version of veterans' benefits is applicable to individuals entering the Army, Navy, Air Force, Marines, or Coast Guard on or after July 1, 1985. Authorized under the Montgomery G.I. Bill, the program differs based on whether the student is on active duty or is in the Reserves.

Benefits for Active Duty

Active duty benefits can be used for the purpose of obtaining a college education while on active duty, after serving at least two years, can be redeemed after separation from the service. In order to be eligible, your child must have a high school diploma or its equivalent before completing the required period of active duty. The serviceperson contributes $100 per month in the form of pay reduction for the first twelve months of active duty. If your child separates from the service, he or she must have received an honorable discharge and must have served either continuously on active duty for three years or for two years followed by four years in the Selected Reserves. Benefits must be used within ten years of discharge. After serving a minimum of two years, your child is entitled to an educational benefit of $23,400 for thirty-six months for full-time study. For three or more years of enlistment, the entitlement increases to $28,800.

Montgomery G.I. Bill Benefits for Selected Reserve Duty

While in the Selected Reserves (Army Reserve, Navy Reserve, Air Force Reserve, Marine Corps Reserve, Coast Guard Reserve, Army National Guard, and Air National Guard), your child can take advantage of educational benefits authorized under the Montgomery G.I. Bill. The service commitment must be for at least six years, and certain eligibility requirements must be met, including having a high school diploma or its equivalent. Your child will not be eligible if he or she already has a bachelor's degree. These benefits are available only during the period of your child's

For more information on veterans' educational benefits, check out www.gibill.va.gov.

participation in the Selected Reserves. Benefits are payable for up to thirty-six months.

Financial Assistance from the Army and Army Reserve

By enlisting in the Army or Army Reserve, your child can either earn money to pay for his or her education or choose to have the Army repay his or her student loans. The following is a summary of the programs sponsored by the Army. The other branches of the military offer similar programs. Your child should contact the recruiter for the branch he or she is interested in for more information.

Army College Fund

If a person scores at least 50 on the Armed Forces Qualification Test (AFQT), he or she may choose an Army job specialty that provides benefits from the Army College Fund, up to $50,000 for college, when combined with Montgomery G.I. Bill benefits. If your child enlists for two years in one of the jobs that offers the Army College Fund, he or she will receive financial assistance for attending college after his or her active-duty term. A three-year enlistment provides a larger benefit and a choice of job specialties. By enlisting for four years in one of the jobs that qualifies for this option, your child receives the largest possible financial benefit. In each case, he or she contributes $100 each month for the first year of enlistment to the Montgomery G.I. Bill fund, for a total contribution of $1,200.

The Army College Fund benefits are paid directly to the student on a monthly basis, with the number of months and the amount received per month based on his or her enrollment status. Other scholarships, grants, or assistance does not affect army benefits. Benefits can be used up to ten years from the date of discharge.

Specialized Training for Army Reserve Readiness (STARR)

Under this program, the Army Reserve pays a maximum of $6000 for tuition, books, and education-related expenses for up to two years to train in selected medical specialties at your child's local college. Note that this program does not cover living expenses. If your child has prior military service, he or she may also be eligible for a bonus.

Because of the shortage of training seats, the Army Reserve pays for study in the following positions:

$ Dental Laboratory Specialist

$ Emergency Medical Technician or Paramedic (no bonus)

$ Licensed Practical Nurse

$ Operating Room Specialist

$ X-ray Specialist

$ Pharmacy Specialist

$ Respiratory Therapy Specialist

Before enlisting, the local Army Reserve recruiter will help your child select and apply to a state-approved college or other educational institution in the chosen medical specialty.

> **If your child does not have prior military experience, he or she must attend basic training during the summer prior to enrollment. He or she must also participate in drills, with pay, one weekend each month during the school year.**

After applying for and receiving the appropriate license for the chosen medical specialty, your child must complete four weeks at an Army medical treatment facility. As a fully trained medical specialist, he or she will then pursue a civilian medical career, while fulfilling his or her obligation in the U.S. Army Reserve. He or she may also participate in the Montgomery G.I. Bill or loan repayment programs.

Army Loan Repayment Program

If your child is a qualified student who has attended college on federal student loans made after October 1, 1975, he or she may choose the Loan Repayment Program upon enlistment in the Army for a minimum three-year term in any job specialty. However, if he or she chooses the repayment option, benefits under the Montgomery G.I. Bill cannot be received. For each year served on active duty, your child's indebtedness is reduced by one third or $1,500, whichever is greater, up to a maximum of $65,000. To be eligible for this program, the loan may not be in default.

In addition to repaying loans borrowed before entry into the service, this program repays student loans incurred while in the service. Loans that qualify for repayment are:

- $ Federal Stafford Loans (subsidized and unsubsidized) and Direct Subsidized and Unsubsidized Loans

- $ Federal Perkins Loans or National Direct Student Loans (NDSL)

- $ Federal PLUS and Federal Direct PLUS Loans

- $ Federal Supplemental Loans for Students (FSLS)

- $ Federal Consolidation and Direct Consolidation Loans (in soldier's name)

To qualify for the Army's Loan Repayment Program, the student must be a high school graduate, have no prior military service, and score at least 50 on the Armed Forces Qualification Test (AFQT).

Army Reserve Student Loan Repayment Program

The same federally funded student loans that qualify for complete repayment with an active duty enlistment also qualify for partial repayment upon enlistment in the Army Reserve. For each year of satisfactory service, the Army Reserve pays 15 percent of the loan amount or $1,500 per year, whichever is greater, up to $10,000. Depending on military occupational specialty, some soldiers may qualify for loan repayments of 15 percent or $3,000 per year, up to $20,000.

Although the loan repayment option must be chosen at the time of enlistment, the Army Reserve repays loans taken out after enlistment. Repayment begins once your child has served one year after securing the loan and has become skill-qualified.

For more information, check out the Army's Web site at www.goarmy.com or contact your nearest Army recruiter.

Servicemember Opportunity College/Community College of the Air Force

Enlisted personnel can also receive degrees through the Community College of the Air Force (CCAF) or the Servicemembers Opportunity College (SOC) of the Army, Navy, Marines, or Coast Guard. These networks enable enlisted men and women to pursue a traditional degree through arrangements with a number of colleges. Participating schools offer flexible academic programs that take into account the unique lifestyle of a servicemember, with its time constraints and pattern of frequent reassignments.

Other military options also exist, such as tuition-free college courses offered by the Navy to personnel on sea duty and credit offered by some institutions for military experience, such as the U.S. Coast Guard Institute. For more information, students and counselors should contact their military recruiters.

To take advantage of one of these opportunities, the serviceperson must be stationed at a base near a college campus that has provided the necessary scheduling for off-duty military personnel. Each base has an education officer who can assist your child if he or she wants to enroll in a local college or take correspondence courses.

Tuition assistance is available in the form of tuition discounts for servicemembers and their families pursuing their education through this network. The military covers 75 to 90 percent of the tuition cost. Your child can take advantage of this program while still in the service and still receive benefits under the G.I. Bill when you get out. Servicemembers and their families can enroll in associate, bachelor, and graduate degree programs through SOC.

Based out of Maxwell Air Force Base in Montgomery, Alabama, CCAF is the largest multi-campus community college in the world. CCAF allows Air Force servicemembers to earn an accredited associate in applied sciences degree in more than sixty educational programs that are directly related to Air Force jobs in the fields of aircraft and missile maintenance, electronics and telecommunications, allied health, logistics and resources, and public and support services. Enlisted personnel must complete their degree program prior to separation, commissioning, or retirement. The Air Force recently opened its CCAF programs to the other branches of the military.

Tuition Assistance Program

The Tuition Assistance (TA) Program provides financial assistance for voluntary off-duty education programs in support of a soldier's professional and personal self-development goals. All soldiers on active duty and all soldiers on selected reserve duty are authorized to participate. Tuition assistance is available for courses that are offered on line, by correspondence or through other nontraditional means. The courses must be offered by colleges that are accredited by accrediting agencies that are recognized by the U.S. Department of Education. Soldiers receive a maximum total yearly amount of up to $3,500 at a rate of 75 percent of tuition costs, or up to $187.50 per semester hour, whichever is less.

Chapter 9

If I Only Knew...

Applying for financial aid can be very daunting, especially if you don't have someone to turn to who has been through it. To help alleviate your apprehensions, Peterson's interviewed five families that went through the financial aid process. Not only do these families share their experiences—both good and bad—they also reveal what they would do differently if they could do it again. If you can learn from their experiences, you will be better able to use the financial aid system to your advantage. Note that we have changed the names of the families to protect their privacy.

THE WEISS FAMILY

Susan Weiss can finally see the light at the end of the tunnel. Of her three children, two have graduated from college, and the third is entering her sophomore year. But what makes this widowed mother's story so amazing is that even though she lives on a fixed income, she sent all three girls to school without the benefit of any financial aid. How? By sending all three to state universities.

Weiss admits that she didn't spend much time looking into financial aid. "I just assumed that if I owned a home and had money in the bank," she says, "I wouldn't be eligible." Her daughters' high school counselors did not offer much guidance regarding financial aid, either. Rather, they helped the girls narrow down their college choices based on what Weiss could afford to spend out-of-pocket.

Of the schools the guidance counselors suggested, Weiss felt the cost of attendance was most reasonable at public schools. So instead of letting her children take out student loans, she encouraged them to focus on public schools in their home state of Pennsylvania. Ultimately, the older daughters enrolled at Penn State and the youngest, Robin, headed for West Chester University.

However, Robin's first choice was the University of Hartford, in Connecticut. Although Hartford sent her an acceptance letter, the cost of tuition, room and board, and fees at the private, out-of-state college proved to be more than Weiss could afford. Knowing how much her daughter wanted to enroll at Hartford, she contacted the school's financial aid office by phone and explained her situation. Weiss also asked her accountant to send the school a follow-up letter. This, however, was probably a mistake, giving the staff at the University of Hartford the impression that Weiss didn't need financial aid as much as she claimed if she could afford an accountant. Ultimately, Robin decided to attend West Chester so she and her mother could avoid taking out loans. "We all have disappointments in life," says Weiss, "but we get over it."

Looking back on her experiences, Weiss regrets that she didn't understand the financial aid process, which meant that her daughters were limited in their choice of colleges. If she had it all to do again, she would do three things differently.

First, she wouldn't have allowed her kids to wait until senior year to look for schools because this limited the number of colleges they were able to consider. Instead, she would have started them early in their junior year so they would have the time to explore a wider range of schools.

Second, Weiss would have taken each of her children to see potential colleges before they sent in their applications—all three girls waited until after they had been accepted to make their college visits.

Finally, Weiss realizes now just how little she knew about the financial aid process. "I should have gone to the colleges and spoken to someone about our options," she says.

THE VERACRUZ FAMILY

Most students rely on their parents to figure out how to get financial aid. But what happens when your parents are immigrants who don't speak much English? "I had to do everything on my own," says Marisol Veracruz.

Veracruz began thinking about financial aid in the middle of her junior year of high school. "My parents make a modest income, and there are two of us going to college at the same time (she has a twin brother), so I knew there was going to be financial aid." Veracruz spent a lot of time in her guidance counselor's office, learning as much as she could about financial aid. Thanks to her counselor, she discovered her home state of New Jersey's Equal Opportunity Fund (EOF). The Fund provides grant money to disadvantaged residents of the state who can demonstrate both financial need and the motivation to pursue higher education.

Veracruz also contacted the financial aid offices of the schools she applied to whenever she had questions. She was surprised by the aid awards she received from New Jersey's Montclair State and Rutgers University. "I didn't think I was going to get all that help money-wise," she says. She chose Rutgers, and in her second year she was again surprised by how large her package was. Besides the EOF, a Perkins loan, and a subsidized loan, Veracruz's aid package includes work-study. "I've gotten $2,000 a year in work-study. That's been helpful." While she has used some of her work-study money to pay bills, Veracruz is saving the majority of it to pay off her loans after graduation.

Veracruz has gone through the application process twice now. "So far, it's gone pretty smoothly," she reflects. And while she wasn't afraid to ask questions of financial aid officers and her high school guidance counselor, she believes the process would have been easier if her parents spoke better English. "They would have supported me more, given me more advice," says Veracruz.

She offers two pieces of advice to families who are applying for financial aid.

$ "The sooner you can start the process," she advises, "the better. If you wait until you're a senior, you're just going to panic."

$ Keep all of your paperwork from each school in a separate file when you're sending out financial aid applications. "As the days went by, I could check to see if I was on the right track."

THE WHITFIELD FAMILY

Barbara Whitfield's daughter Tiffany had high SAT scores, strong grades, and plenty of extracurricular activities. "Everything," says Whitfield, "that you were supposed to do to get all the money you could get. We expected the world to open up and give her everything."

At first the Whitfields were thrilled when Tiffany received merit awards from Lehigh and Lafayette Universities. But the awards—$3,000 per year—were not enough to make a significant difference. Tuition, room and board, fees, and transportation costs were going to total nearly $30,000 a year. Whitfield says that when you're looking at such a large expense, "It's not about what the college is giving you, it's about what you have left to pay."

The Whitfields took the next natural step: They applied for need-based aid. Whitfield and her husband were proud that they had paid off the mortgage on their home a few years earlier. But every financial aid officer the Whitfields spoke to had the same response: "For the equity that you have in the house, you can send three children to this school." Need-based aid would not be available to them. In the end, the Whitfields took out a home equity loan in order to send their daughter to college. Rather than be bitter about it, though, Whitfield says, "You owe your child an education, so you need to put in some of your own money to show your child the value of it."

To offset costs, Whitfield had several recommendations.

$ Look into private scholarships. "There are a lot of scholarships out there—religious, cultural, heritage affiliations—but you have to search them out."

$ Look into private schools that offer tuition reductions. Because of Tiffany's strong SAT score, Rider University offered to knock enough off the top to make tuition and room and board equal to that of a state university. "But parents beware," she warns, "if your child does not maintain an academic average, you lose it all!"

$ Don't rush to pay off your house. It isn't worth it.

THE DELVETTO FAMILY

Annie Delvetto's son Tommy received aid packages from ten different colleges. So when the Delvettos sat down to compare the awards, they quickly realized that they had to get organized. "You can't just look at the numbers and go from paper to paper," she says. "You have to actually put it up on a computer screen and look at the college, the tuition, the room and board."

The Delvettos, who live in New Jersey, initially were impressed by the large package offered by a well-known private university in Massachusetts. "But people fail to take into consideration all the extra expenses that go along with college," says Delvetto. "Everyone seems to think that the amount of money in the college guide is what it's going to cost. They don't add up all the other little incidentals that come along." These oft-forgotten costs include traveling home for the holidays and visits, parents' weekend, and medical expenses. "When you factor those things in," says Delvetto, "you have to look at a different picture than the school that is just 10 minutes away."

Delvetto and her husband Paul went through the financial aid process with two other children a decade ago. But when it came time to apply for Tommy, they discovered that things had changed dramatically. "More forms to fill out, they ask you more questions, they ask for what your children have in their savings accounts. They don't make the financial aid process 'people-friendly.'" Realizing how critical it is to understand the questions that are asked on the financial aid forms, the Delvettos hired a financial aid adviser.

And when it came time to compare aid packages, the Delvettos created a spreadsheet on their home computer with three types of columns: expenses (tuition, room and board, and transportation); aid (subsidized and unsubsidized loans, work-study, and scholarships); and unmet need. "Nothing overwhelming," says Delvetto, who used her spreadsheet to help her son choose Villanova. You don't even need to create it on a computer. A pen and a piece of paper work just as well.

Annie Delvetto has the following advice for parents.

$ A financial adviser is not worth the cost. Instead, she recommends organizing yourself by making a binder for each school you're interested in.

$ Visit each school's financial aid office.

$ Write down your impressions about each school after each visit—"otherwise you will start mixing up who said what and how much he said."

THE REYNOLDS FAMILY

When it comes to finding financial aid, you might think that Bob Reynolds has an advantage over most families because he's an accountant. It turns out, though, that the opposite is true. "I didn't know what to expect," he says of applying for aid for his stepdaughter. But it didn't take long before he learned "to forget the government unless you're at the poverty level, except for loans." Reynolds's experience has shown him that middle-class families who own a home and make a living that allows them to raise a family comfortably won't get much federal assistance.

Reynolds's stepdaughter was open to both public and private schools, and no specific school stood out as a "first choice." Instead, the final decision of where she would go to college would depend on the financial aid packages she received. As an accountant, Reynolds has seen his share of families who take out large loans to put their kids through college. "But I didn't want she or I saddled with a lot of debt," he recalls. So Reynolds went to work securing private scholarship money for his stepdaughter. Of the fifteen private and state scholarship programs his stepdaughter applied to, she only won one, what Reynolds calls an obscure, random state scholarship. "There's probably a lot more out there than people realize," he says, but he regrets that he had a difficult time locating legitimate scholarship programs.

The Reynolds had to rely primarily on institutional financial aid and knew that they would have a better chance at winning scholarship money from colleges that most people have never heard of. So they applied to four small schools in Massachusetts, including Regis College. Once acceptance letters arrived, Reynolds got in touch with the financial aid offices by phone to negotiate aid packages. "If the college wants you," advises Reynolds, "they'll find something for you."

He found the staff at Regis to be "very pleasant" in the three or four calls he placed. And because it was a small school, each time he dealt with the same two people, one of whom was the school's financial aid director. Ultimately, he and Regis negotiated "a very nice package," says Reynolds. Regis offered his stepdaughter two grants based on academic performance, an off-campus work-study placement, and a subsidized Stafford Loan. "The first year," Reynolds recalls, "50 percent was covered, tuition and board." The remaining costs were made more manageable with a monthly payment plan.

Reynolds is about to start the process again with his son, a high school junior. What will he do differently this time? "I'm starting earlier, looking at potential colleges that meet his needs." Also, Reynolds will encourage his son to apply to more schools and to visit more colleges for face-to-face interviews in the hopes of securing better financial aid packages.

His advice to other families is simple.

$ "Find those schools that not everyone is applying to." There are hundreds of small colleges out there that families pass over because they aren't the most popular or prestigious. What people don't realize is that these schools are the ones that are willing to make some concessions so the cost of higher education is affordable to middle-class families.

Chapter 10

Repaying Student Loans

Written by American Education Services (AES)

STUDENT LOAN COMMITMENT

As your child heads off to college, there are many things that you may be thinking about (and worrying about) right now. You've probably been very focused on choosing the right school, applying for admission, and finding financial aid. Then you'll have the next four years or more to get through, depending on if your son or daughter goes on to graduate school. The last thing on your mind is the repayment of student loans. As a parent, however, it is important that you help your child understand the commitment that must be made when taking out a student loan.

Although the word "commitment" may give you second thoughts, realize that loans are necessary for many students to open the door to higher education and a brighter future. It is important to encourage your child to seek gift aid first, such as grants and scholarships, and then finance the remaining cost of his or her education via student loans.

Your child should also consider the cost of repayment when considering a student loan. Most student loans are repaid at a monthly rate over a period of ten years. It would be helpful for you to work with your child to determine a realistic income in their anticipated career. The Career Planning module at www.aesmentor.org will help you with this task. With this information on hand, it will be easier to decide on the amount that he or she will be comfortable borrowing and repaying. Tables providing various interest rates are available from lending institutions and at the financial aid office of the school your student is considering attending.

> By offering your child a student loan, whether Perkins, FFEL, Direct, or alternative, the school or lender trusts that your child will fulfill his or her obligation and repay the amount in full.

REPAYMENT BASICS

If it is determined that a student loan is necessary to fund your child's education, there are some important things you need to know about repayment. Here are some commonly asked questions about repaying student loans and answers that will give you the tips you need when it comes time for your child to repay his or her student loan:

$ **What is a grace period?** A grace period is allotted to loan borrowers, during which time they do not need to begin repaying their loan. In the case of a Stafford loan, the grace period is typically six months after he finishes school or drops below half-time enrollment. However, if the loan is subsidized, repayment can begin during the grace period. Those payments will be applied directly to the principal of the loan, allowing   pay off of the loan sooner than expected.

$ **Is a student loan legally binding?** A Master Promissory Note (MPN) must be signed in order to borrow money for financing higher education. This legally binding document obligates your child to repay the loan as stated in the terms and conditions of the MPN.

$ **Are there benefits to repayment?** A student loan is "necessary debt"; without it a borrower would not be able to finance his or her education. If, after graduation, your son or daughter meets this obligation and makes monthly payments on the loan, your child will earn a good credit rating that will provide lifelong benefits.

$ **What if my child decides to go on to graduate school?** Should your child decide to go on to graduate school, any student loan financing used to fund undergraduate schooling will be deferred until graduation from grad school.

$ **What are the payment methods for making student loan payments?** There are several options in making payments on student loans. In most cases, your child will be offered the opportunity to make payments on line, mail in checks, or participate in an automatic debit program in which payments are withdrawn from a designated bank account on a monthly basis.

Enrolling in an automatic debit program will, in most cases, also earn a .25 percent interest rate reduction. Check with the loan holder to learn what repayment benefits apply in your child's case.

$ **What if my child is having a hard time making loan payments?** There are several repayment scheduling options available:

> $ *Standard Repayment Schedule:* Payments are the same each month but may be adjusted each year to reflect the variable interest rate. Total repayment schedule is ten years.

> $ *Graduated Repayment Schedule:* Smaller monthly payments are made early in the repayment schedule and larger payments later in the schedule. Total repayment schedule is ten years.

> $ *Income-Sensitive Repayment Schedule:* Loan payments are based on monthly income. Total repayment term may be extended beyond ten years.

$ **What if my child misses a payment?** One missed payment will not place your child's loan into default. However, it will appear on his or her credit record and may affect his or her ability to obtain additional credit. If it is not possible to make a payment, your child should contact the servicer of the loan and explain the situation. In some cases, your child may be eligible for a deferment or forbearance. The worst thing the borrower can do is miss the payment or become habitually late in making payments.

$ **What is a student loan deferment?** Deferment is an authorized temporary suspension of repayment. This may be granted under certain circumstances that must be discussed with the holder of the loan. A deferment is not automatic; borrowers must apply, meet certain qualifications, and make arrangements with the holder of the loan. Until notified regarding eligibility for deferment, borrowers should continue making up-to-date payments.

$ What is forbearance? A student loan forbearance allows the borrower to reduce the amount of his or her student loan payment or temporarily stop making payments. However, interest continues to accrue during a forbearance period. If your child is financially unable to make payments under the terms of the repayment schedule, a request of forbearance can be made for:

$ A short period during which no payment is made.

$ An extension of time for making payments.

$ A period in which smaller payments are made than were originally scheduled.

$ Can anyone get a forbearance? Unlike a student loan deferment, a forbearance is granted at the discretion of the servicer of the loans. However the loan holder must grant a forbearance upon receipt of the reason for the request and paper documentation if:

$ The borrower is a dental or medical intern.

$ The monthly student loan payments equal or exceed 20 percent of the borrower's monthly income.

$ The borrower is serving in a national service position.

$ The borrower qualifies under the Student Loan Repayment Program administered by the U.S. Department of Defense.

$ The borrower is affected by a local or national emergency.

$ The borrower is a member of the National Guard or Reserves and is mobilized.

$ The borrower resides in a designated disaster area.

$ What are the consequences if my child does not repay a loan? The consequences for nonrepayment are very serious, having a long-term effect on your child's life.

$ Your child may not be able to obtain more credit, for example, to buy a car or house.

$ Your child may be turned down for a credit card.

$ Your child could forfeit his or her tax refunds.

$ Your child's employer can be ordered to withhold what he or she owes from his or her paycheck.

$ Your child may be sued, owe collection and attorney fees, and still be responsible for repaying the loan.

$ **Is loan consolidation a good idea if my child has to take out more than one loan?** It may be easier to repay several loans at one time by consolidating them into one monthly payment that can be extended up to thirty years. Although the monthly payment can be lower, borrowers may pay a larger amount of total interest. In some cases, the interest rate on a consolidation loan may be higher than the rates on the original loans. Before consolidating loans, contact the loan representative to make sure that loan consolidation would be in your child's best interest.

> **With consolidation, it is important to shop around for the best offer. Read all of the details carefully; you don't want your child to end up paying more or for a longer period of time than necessary.**

$ **When should borrowers contact their loan holder?** During school, borrowers should contact their loan holder if there are any changes in name, address, telephone number, or enrollment status. Afterward, borrowers are required to inform the holder when they graduate, leave school, or drop below half-time enrollment status. During repayment, borrowers should inform the loan holder of a change in name, address, or telephone number. It is important to notify the holder if the payments cannot be made or if payments will be late.

Your child should have no problem meeting the responsibilities of student loan repayment if he or she sticks to a realistic budget and works with the loan holder to create a payment schedule that works. The best repayment strategy is to schedule monthly payments as high as his or her budget will allow, without endangering the possibility of making those payments.

Although a student loan is ultimately your child's responsibility, we know that it often falls to the parent to reiterate the importance of that commitment while planning for college. We wish you and your child luck as you prepare for postsecondary education!

Glossary

Ability to Benefit: Postsecondary institutions may not award federal aid to students without a high school or equivalency diploma unless the student has demonstrated that he or she can benefit from the education offered. *See page 41*

Academic Credit: The unit of measurement an institution gives to a student when he/she fulfills course or subject requirement(s) as determined by the institution.

Academic Year (AY): This is a measure of the academic work to be accomplished by a student. The school defines its own academic year, but the federal regulations set minimum standards to determine federal financial aid awards. For instance, the academic year must be at least 30 weeks of instructional time in which a full-time student is expected to complete at least 24 semester or trimester credit hours or 36 quarter credit hours or 900 clock hours.

Adjusted Available Income: The portion of family income remaining after deducting federal, state, and local taxes, a living allowance, and other factors used in the Federal Need Analysis Methodology. *See page 109*

Adjusted Gross Income (AGI): All taxable income as reported on a U.S. income tax return.

Advanced Placement (AP) Program: A series of examinations demonstrating a student's proficiency in a subject area, for which some postsecondary institutions offer credit. *See page 137*

AmeriCorps: *See National and Community Service.*

Assets: Cash on hand in checking and savings accounts; trusts, stocks, bonds, other securities; real estate (excluding home), income-producing property, business equipment, and business inventory. Considered in determining Expected Family Contribution (EFC) under the regular formula.

Associate Degree: A degree given for successful completion of some courses of study at a two-year college.

Award Letter: A means of notifying successful financial aid applicants of the assistance being offered. The award letter usually provides information on the types and amounts of aid offered, as well as specific program information, student responsibilities, and the conditions that govern the award. Generally provides students with the opportunity to accept or decline the aid offered. *See page 128–129*

Award Year: The period of time between July 1 of one year and June 30 of the following year.

Bachelor's Degree: The degree given for successful completion of the undergraduate curriculum at a four-year college or a university. Also called baccalaureate degree.

Base Year: For need analysis purposes, the base year is the 12-month calendar year preceding the award year (e.g., 2001 is the base year for the 2002–2003 award year).

BIA Grant: *See Bureau of Indian Affairs Grant.*

Bureau of Indian Affairs (BIA) Grant: A federal grant program administered by the Bureau of Indian Affairs for needy students who are enrolled members of an Indian, Eskimo, or Aleut tribe and enrolled in accredited institutions in pursuit of an undergraduate or graduate degree. *See page 59*

Business Assets: Property that is used in the operation of a trade or business, including real estate, inventories, buildings, machinery and other equipment, patents, franchise rights, and copyrights. Considered in determining a family's expected contribution (EFC) under the regular formula.

Campus-based Programs: The term commonly applied to those U.S. Department of Education federal student aid programs administered directly by institutions of postsecondary education. Includes: Federal Supplemental Educational Opportunity Grant (FSEOG), Federal Work-Study (FWS), and Federal Perkins Loan programs. *See pages 44–45*

Cancellation (of loan): The condition that exists when a borrower of a federal student loan has fulfilled requirements to permit cancellation of, or writing off of, a designated portion of the principal and interest. *See page 53*

Capitalization (of interest): When interest payments are deferred and added to the principal amount of the loan.

Certificate: The formal acknowledgment of successful completion of a particular program or course of study, particularly in a vocational school, trade school, or junior college.

Citizen: A person who owes allegiance to the United States. Most state and federal financial aid programs are considered domestic assistance programs and are available only to citizens, nationals, permanent residents of the U.S., and people who are in this country for other than temporary purposes. Citizens of the Republic of Marshall Islands, the Federated States of Micronesia, and Republic of Palau are eligible for Federal Pell Grant, FSEOG and FWS only. *See page 40*

CLEP: *See College-Level Examination Program.*

Clock Hour: The unit of measurement some institutions give for fulfilling course requirements.

COA: *See Cost of Attendance.*

College-Level Examination Program (CLEP): A series of examinations demonstrating a student's proficiency in a subject area, for which some postsecondary institutions offer credit. *See page 138*

Commercial Lender: A commercial bank, savings and loan association, credit union, stock savings bank, trust company, or mutual savings bank. Can act as a lender for the Federal Family Education Loan (FFEL) Program. *See page 47*

Commuter Student: A student who does not live on campus; typically, commuter refers to a student living at home with his or her parents, but can also mean any student who lives off-campus.

Consolidation Loan: A loan made to enable a borrower with different types of loans to obtain a single loan with one interest rate and one repayment schedule. Federal Perkins, Federal Stafford (subsidized and unsubsidized), Direct Loan, Health Education Assistance Loans (HEAL), Health Professions Student Loans, and Loans for Disadvantaged Students may be combined for purposes of consolidation, subject to certain eligibility requirements. A consolidation loan pays off the existing loans; the borrower repays the consolidated loan. *See page 163*

Cost of Attendance (COA): In general, this includes the tuition and fees normally assessed a student, together with the institutions estimate of the cost of room and board, transportation and commuting costs, books and supplies, and miscellaneous personal expenses. In addition, student loan fees, dependent care, reasonable costs for a study abroad or cooperative education program, and/or costs related to a disability may be included, when appropriate. Also referred to as cost of education or budget. *See page 38*

Credit (or Credit Hour): The unit of measurement some institutions give for fulfilling course requirements.

DANTES: *See Defense Activity for Non-Traditional Education Support.*

Default (Federal Perkins Loan): A loan for which the borrower failed to make an installment payment when due and such failure persisted (not cured either by payment or other appropriate arrangements). The Department of Education considers a loan discharged in bankruptcy not to be in default.

Default (Federal Stafford, Direct, Federal PLUS, or Direct PLUS Loans): The failure of a borrower to make an installment payment when due, or to meet other terms of the promissory note under circumstances where the Secretary of Education or the pertinent guaranty agency finds it reasonable to conclude that the borrower no longer intends to honor the obligation to repay. The Department of Education considers a loan discharged in bankruptcy not to be in default.

Defense Activity for Non-Traditional Education Support (DANTES): A series of examinations sponsored by the military to help service men and women as well as non-military people obtain college credit for the knowledge and skills they have acquired. *See page 139*

Deferment (of loan): A condition during which payments of principal are not required, and, for Federal Perkins and Federal Subsidized Stafford and Direct Subsidized Loans, interest does not accrue. The repayment period is extended by the length of the deferment period. *See page 47*

Department of Education, U.S. (ED): The section of the federal government that administers assistance to students enrolled in postsecondary educational programs under the following programs: Federal Pell Grant, Federal Perkins Loan, Federal Supplemental Educational Opportunity Grant (FSEOG), Federal Work-Study (FWS), Federal Family Education Loan (FFEL), and William D. Ford Federal Direct Loan. *See pages 39–56*

Departmental Scholarship: An award of gift assistance that is specifically designated for a recipient in a particular academic department within the institution. *See page 61*

Direct Loan (Subsidized and Unsubsidized): Long term, low-interest loans administered by the Department of Education and institutions. Variable interest rate not to exceed 8.25 percent. Direct Unsubsidized Loans can be used to replace EFC. *See page 56*

Disbursement: The process by which financial aid funds are made available to students for use in meeting educational and related living expenses. *See page 131*

ED: *See Department of Education, U.S.*

Educational Benefits: Funds, primarily federal, awarded to certain categories of students (veterans, children of deceased veterans or other deceased wage earners, and students with physical disabilities) to help finance their postsecondary education regardless of their ability to demonstrate need in the traditional sense.

Educational Expenses: *See Cost of Attendance.*

EFC: *See Expected Family Contribution.*

Eligibility Criteria: The specific conditions that a student must meet to qualify for financial assistance. In addition to demonstrating need for most programs, general eligibility criteria for federal student aid include, among other things, citizenship status and selective service registration. Individual programs may carry other specific eligibility requirements in addition to the general eligibility criteria. *See pages 40–43*

Eligible Institution: An institution of higher education, vocational school, postsecondary vocational institution, or proprietary institution of higher education that meets all criteria for participation in the federal student aid programs.

Eligible Noncitizen: Person who, although not a U.S. citizen, qualifies for federal student aid in one of the following eligible categories: 1) U.S. Permanent resident who has an Alien Registration Receipt Card (Form I-151, I-551, usually referred to as green cards) or other evidence of admission for permanent residence; 2) Conditional permanent resident (I-151C); 3) Person designated as lawfully present in U.S. for other than a temporary purpose who has an Arrival-Departure Record (Form I-94) from INS stamped as refugee, granted asylum, indefinite parolee and/or humanitarian parolee, or Cuban-Haitian entrant; 5) Permanent residents of the Republic of Palau or citizens of the Republic of the Marshall Islands and the Federated States of Micronesia. Non-citizens who are not eligible for federal student aid include holders of Student Visas, Exchange Visitors Visas, G-Series Visas, or those who have only a Notice of Approval to Apply for Permanent Residence. *See page 40*

Eligible Program: A program of education or training that leads to a degree or a certificate at a school participating in one or more federal student aid programs. A student must be enrolled in an eligible program at an eligible school to receive federal student assistance.

Employment: With reference to financial aid, the opportunity for students to earn money to help pay for their education. Federal Work-Study is one program by which needy students can work to defray their educational expenses. *See page 45*

Endowment: Funds obtained and owned by the postsecondary institution that are invested so that the income from the investment can be used for various purposes such as construction, research, and financial aid.

Enrolled: The completion of registration requirements (other than the payment of tuition and fees) at the institution the student is or will be attending; a correspondence school student must be accepted for admission and complete and submit one lesson to be considered enrolled.

Enrollment Status: At those institutions using semesters, trimesters, quarters, or other academic terms and measuring progress by credit hours, enrollment status equals a students credit hour workload categorized as either full-time, three-quarter-time, half-time, or less-than-half-time.

Entitlement Program: Program that is funded sufficiently to ensure that all eligible applicants are guaranteed to receive maximum authorized awards. As long as the student applicant meets all the eligibility requirements and is enrolled in an eligible program at an eligible institution, he or she will receive the award for which eligibility has been established.

Expected Family Contribution (EFC): The amount a student and his or her family are expected to pay toward the students cost of attendance as calculated by a Congressionally mandated formula known as Federal Methodology. The EFC is used to determine a student's eligibility for the student financial assistance programs. *See pages 37 and 107*

FAFSA: *See Free Application for Federal Student Aid.*

FAFSA Processor: An organization contracted by the Department of Education to provide the means for a student to apply for federal student aid. The FAFSA processor electronically enters the students FAFSA data into a computer system and then transmits the data to the Central Processing System.

Federal Family Education Loan (FFEL) Program: The collective name for the Federal Stafford (subsidized and unsubsidized), Federal PLUS Loan, and Federal Consolidated Loan programs. Funds for these programs are provided by private lenders and the loans are guaranteed by the federal government. *See page 47*

Federal Methodology (FM): *See Federal Need Analysis Methodology.*

Federal Need Analysis Methodology: A standardized method for determining a students ability to pay for postsecondary education expenses; also referred to as Federal Methodology (FM). The single formula for determining an Expected Family Contribution (EFC) for Pell Grants, campus-based programs, FFEL program, and Direct Loan program; the formula is defined in statute. *See pages 108–111*

Federal Pell Grant: A federal grant program for needy postsecondary students who have not yet received a baccalaureate or first professional degree; administered by the U.S. Department of Education. *See pages 43–44*

Federal Perkins Loan: One of the campus-based programs; a long term, low interest loan program for both undergraduate and graduate students at a current interest rate of 5%. *See pages 46–47*

Federal Stafford Loan (subsidized and unsubsidized): Long-term, low-interest loans administered by the Department of Education through private guarantee agencies. Formerly known as Guaranteed Student Loans (GSLs). Variable interest rate, not to exceed 8.25%. Federal Unsubsidized Stafford Loans may be used to replace EFC. *See pages 48–53*

Federal Supplemental Educational Opportunity Grant (FSEOG): One of the campus-based programs; grants to undergraduate students of exceptional financial need who have not completed their first baccalaureate degree and who are financially in need of this grant to enable them to pursue their education. Priority for FSEOG awards must be given to Federal Pell Grant recipients with the lowest EFCs. *See page 45*

Federal Work-Study Program (FWS): One of the campus-based programs; a part-time employment program that provides jobs for undergraduate and graduate students who are in need of such earnings to meet a portion of their educational expenses. *See page 45*

FFELP: *See Federal Family Education Loan Programs.*

Financial Aid: General term that describes any source of student assistance outside the student or the students family. Funds awarded to a student to help meet postsecondary educational expenses. These funds are generally awarded on the basis of financial need and include scholarships, grants, loans, and employment.

Financial Aid Administrator: An individual who is responsible for preparing and communicating information pertaining to student loans, grants or scholarships, and employment programs, and for advising, awarding, reporting, counseling, and supervising office functions related to student financial aid. He/she is accountable to the various publics that are involved, is a manager or administrator who interprets and implements federal, state, and institutional policies and regulations, and is capable of analyzing student and employee needs and making changes where necessary.

Financial Aid Award: An offer of financial or in-kind assistance to a student attending a postsecondary educational institution. This award may be in the form of one or more of the following types of financial aid: repayable loan, a non-repayable grant and/or scholarship, and/or student employment.

Financial Aid Consultant: A person who, for a fee, provides a variety of services to students, including preparing the FAFSA and other financial aid forms, estimating the Expected Family Contribution (EFC), and estimating financial need.

Financial Aid Notification: The letter from the postsecondary institution that lets the student know whether or not aid has been awarded. If the student will be receiving assistance, the notification also describes the financial aid package. State agencies and private organizations may send students financial aid notifications separately from the postsecondary institution. Also see Award Letter.

Financial Aid Package: A financial aid award to a student comprised of a combination of forms of financial aid (loans, grants and/or scholarships, employment). *See page 119*

Financial Aid Transcript (FAT): Provides a students financial aid history needed to monitor certain aspects of student eligibility. This information is reported on SARs and ISIRs or schools can access a students financial aid history electronically through the National Student Loan Data System (NSLDS). In some cases, a school may require you to obtain a paper FAT. *See page 41*

Financial Need: The difference between the institutions cost of attendance and the family's ability to pay (i.e., Expected Family Contribution). Ability to pay is represented by the Expected Family Contribution for federal need-based aid and for many state and institutional programs.

Financial Need Equation: Cost of attendance minus Expected Family Contribution equals financial need (COA – EFC = Need). *See page 37*

FM: *See Federal Need Analysis Methodology.*

Forbearance: Permitting the temporary cessation of repayments of loans, allowing an extension of time for making loan payments, or accepting smaller loan payments than were previously scheduled. *See page 162*

Foreign Student: A student belonging to or owing allegiance to another country. Foreign students are not eligible for the basic federal programs, although there are categories of non-U.S. citizens who owe permanent allegiance to the United States and are eligible for student aid.

Formula: *See Need Analysis Formula.*

Free Application for Federal Student Aid (FAFSA): The financial aid application document completed by the student that collects household and financial information. The FAFSA is the foundation document for all federal need analysis computations and database matches performed for a student. *See page 102*

FSEOG: *See Federal Supplemental Educational Opportunity Grant.*

Full-time Student: In general, one who is taking a minimum of 12 semester or quarter hours per academic term; 24 semester or 36 quarter hours per year at institutions using credits but not terms; or 24 clock hours per week at institutions that measure progress in clock hours.

Gift Aid: Educational funds such as grants or scholarships that do not require repayment from present or future earnings. *See pages 65–76*

Grace Period: The period of time that begins when a loan recipient ceases to be enrolled at least half-time and ends when the repayment period starts. Loan principal need not be paid and, generally, interest does not accrue during this period. *See pages 46, 160*

Grant: A type of financial aid that does not have to be repaid; usually awarded on the basis of need, possibly combined with some skills or characteristics the student possesses. *Also see Gift Aid.*

Health and Human Services, U.S. Department of (HHS): The section of the federal government that provides assistance to future health care practitioners. The Nursing Student Loan, Health Profession Student Loan, and Scholarships for Disadvantaged Students Program are among some of the aid programs administered by HHS. *See pages 56–59*

Health Professions Programs: Federal student assistance programs administered by the U.S. Department of Health and Human Services for students preparing for careers in the health sciences. *See pages 57–59*

Health Professions Student Loan (HPSL): A long term, low interest loan program designed to assist students in specific health professions disciplines. *See page 58*

HHS: *See Health and Human Services, U.S. Department of.*

Hope Scholarship: A federal tax credit for higher education expenses *See pages 9, 98, and 141*

Income: Amount of money received from any or all of the following: wages, interest, dividends, sales or rental of property or services, business or farm profits, certain welfare programs, and subsistence allowances such as taxable and non-taxable social security benefits and child support.

Income Protection Allowance: An allowance against income for the basic costs of maintaining family members in the home. The allowance is based upon consumption and other cost estimates of the Bureau of Labor Statistics for a family at the low standard of living.

Independent Student: A student who: (a) will be 24 years of age by December 31, 1999, or who (b) is an orphan; or a ward of the court; (c) is a veteran; (d) is married or is a graduate or professional student; (e) has legal dependents other than a spouse; or (f) presents documentation of other unusual circumstances demonstrating independence to the student financial aid administrator.

Institutional Costs: Charges for tuition, fees, institutionally owned or operated room and board, and other educationally related charges assessed by the institution.

Institutional Student Information Record (ISIR): Output document or information that a school receives by participating in the electronic data exchange process. Contains the results of the FAFSA a student filed, whether it was filed on paper or electronically. Electronic version of the SAR. *See page 106*

Investment Plans: Educational savings programs, usually sponsored by commercial banking institutions. *See pages 1–6*

ISIR: *See Institutional Student Information Record.*

Legal Dependent: A biological or adopted child, or a person for whom the applicant has been appointed legal guardian, and for whom the applicant provides more than half support. In addition, a person who lives with and receives at least half support from the applicant and will continue to receive that support during the award year.

Legal Resident: A person who has met a state or local districts requirements for being declared a resident. May also refer to an individual who is not a U.S. citizen but is still eligible for federal financial aid funds. *See Eligible Noncitizen and Residency Requirements.*

Lifetime Learning Tax Credit: A federal tax credit for higher education expenses. *See pages 9, 98, and 141*

Loan: An advance of funds that is evidenced by a promissory note requiring the recipient to repay the specified amount(s) under prescribed conditions.

Loan Repayment Program: A special program available to qualified students who have attended college on federally funded student loans and who subsequently enlist in the Army for at least three years in a job specialty. *See page 146*

Merit-based Aid: Student assistance awarded because of a student's achievement or talent in a particular area, such as academics, athletics, music, etc.

Methodology: Refers to the system used to calculate the Expected Family Contribution (i.e., the Federal Need Analysis Methodology).

Military Scholarships: Reserve Officer Training Corps (ROTC) scholarships available for the Army, Navy, and Air Force at many colleges and universities throughout the United States. These scholarships cover tuition and fees, books and supplies, and include a subsistence allowance.

Montgomery GI Bill: A program to help military personnel pay for postsecondary education. Sometimes called the New GI Bill. *See page 144*

National and Community Service (AmeriCorps): A program established through the National and Community Service Trust Act of 1993 designed to reward individuals who provide community service with educational benefits and/or loan forgiveness or cancellation. *See pages 10 and 143*

National Health Service Corps Scholarship (NHSC): Scholarship program for students who pursue full-time courses of study in certain health professions disciplines, and are willing to serve as primary care practitioners in underserved areas after completing their education. *See page 58*

National Student Loan Data System (NSLDS): A national database of Title IV loan information and selected federal grant data.

Need: *See Financial Need.*

Need Analysis: A system by which a student applicant's ability to pay for educational expenses is evaluated and calculated. Need analysis consists of two primary components: (a) determination of an estimate of the applicants and/or family's ability to contribute to educational expenses; and (b) determination of an accurate estimate of the educational expenses themselves. *See page 107*

Need Analysis Formula: Defines the data elements used to calculate the Expected Family Contribution (EFC); there are two distinct formulas: regular and simplified. The formula determines the EFC under the Federal Need Analysis Methodology. *See page 108*

Need-based Aid: Student assistance awarded because a students financial circumstances would not permit him or her to afford the cost of a postsecondary education.

Need Equation: *See Financial Need Equation.*

Non-Need-Based Aid: Aid based on criteria other than need, such as academic, musical, or athletic ability. Also, refers to federal student aid programs where the Expected Family Contribution (EFC) is not part of the need equation.

Noninstitutional Costs: Costs associated with postsecondary attendance that are not assessed by the institution, such as off-campus room and board, books, supplies, transportation, and other miscellaneous personal expenses.

Notification: *See Award Letter and Financial Aid Notification.*

Nursing Student Loan (NSL): Loans available to nursing students attending approved nursing schools offering a diploma, or associate, baccalaureate, or graduate degree in nursing. *See page 57*

Out-of-State Student: As defined by a public institution, a student who is not a legal resident of the state or local district that is legislatively and fiscally responsible for supervision of that institution; generally, such students are assessed higher tuition rates than those for legal residents. Also referred to as non-resident students.

Overaward: A situation in which the students combined resources, including Expected Family Contribution (EFC) and financial aid, are greater than the cost of attendance. Within certain tolerance levels, overawards are not permitted for students receiving federal student assistance funds.

Packaging: The process of combining various types of student aid (grants, loans, scholarships, and employment) to attempt to meet full amount of students need. *See page 117*

Packaging Philosophy: The postsecondary institutions rationale for combining different types of aid to meet a students need. This varies from school to school. *See page 117*

Part-time Student: One who attends an institution on a less than-full-time basis as defined by the institution.

Portability: An attribute of certain student aid programs that allows an eligible student to receive funds from any eligible institution rather than one specific institution. Applies to Federal Pell Grant, as well as to some state scholarships that students may use at postsecondary institutions, including those located outside the state awarding the funds. *See page 44*

Prepayment Penalty: The charge the lender assesses to borrowers who repay a loan faster than the maximum repayment period stated in the promissory note. Federal loan programs do not have prepayment penalties.

Principal (of a loan): The amount of money borrowed through a loan; does not include interest or other charges, unless they are capitalized.

Privacy Acts: Those collective statutes that serve to protect an individual from the release of specified data without the individuals prior written consent.

Projected Year Income: Income expected to be received during the first calendar year of the award year; may also be some other 12-month period.

Promissory Note: The legal document that binds a borrower to the repayment obligations and other terms and conditions that govern a loan program. *See page 160*

Reauthorization: A congressional review process intended to refine authorized federal programs to ensure they continue to meet the needs of the populations they are intended to serve.

Regular Student: A person who is enrolled or accepted for enrollment at an institution of higher education for the purpose of obtaining a degree, certificate, or other recognized educational credential offered by the institution.

Renewal FAFSA: One type of FAFSA that resembles a SAR and bears the same questions as the FAFSA. The Renewal FAFSA is preprinted with the students prior year responses to certain data items that are likely to remain constant from year to year. *See page 102*

Repayment Schedule: A plan that should be provided to the borrower at the time he or she ceases at least half-time study. The plan should set forth the principal and interest due on each installment and the number of payments required to pay the loan in full. In addition, it should include the interest rate, the due date of the first payment, and the frequency of payments. *See pages 160–161*

Reserve Officer Training Corps Scholarship Program: *See ROTC Scholarship Program.*

Residency Requirement: Criteria students must meet to be considered residents of a state or district; used in some cases to determine tuition charges.

Resources: Resources include, but are not limited to, any: (a) funds the student is entitled to receive from a Federal Pell Grant; (b) waiver of tuition and fees; grants, including FSEOG and ROTC subsistence allowances; (d) scholarships, including athletic and ROTC scholarships; (e) need-based fellowships or assistantships; (f) insurance programs for the students education; (g) long term loans made by the institution, including Federal Perkins and Direct Loans; (h) earnings from need-based employment; (i) veterans benefits; and (j) any portion of other long term loans, including Stafford (GSL) Loans, FPLUS, Direct PLUS, state-sponsored, or private loans, not used as a substitute for the EFC.

ROTC Scholarship Program: Competitive scholarship that pays for tuition, fees, books and a monthly living stipend and other benefits in exchange for participating in drills and classes during the academic year, military camp during the summer, and, upon graduation, full-time active duty in the military for at least four years.

SAR: *See Student Aid Report.*

SAR Information Acknowledgment: A non-correctable one-page Student Aid Report containing Part I only. Students who file electronic applications or who make electronic corrections to applicant information through a school receive this acknowledgment. *See page 105*

Satisfactory Academic Progress: The progress required of a financial aid recipient in acceptable studies or other activities to fulfill a specified educational objective.

Scholarship: A form of financial assistance that does not require repayment or employment and is usually made to students who demonstrate or show potential for distinction, usually in academic performance.

Scholarships for Disadvantaged Students (SDS): A federal scholarship program designed to assist disadvantaged students enrolled in certain health profession disciplines. *See page 58*

Scholarship Search Services: Organizations that claim to help students find little known and unused financial aid funds. Families who are interested in using such a service should carefully investigate the company first. *See pages 76–81*

School Year: *See Academic Year.*

Self-help Aid: Funds provided through the work and effort of the student, including savings from past earnings, income from current earnings, or a loan to be repaid from future earnings.

Self-help Expectation: The assumption that a student has an obligation to help pay for a portion of his/her education.

Service Academy: The five postsecondary institutions administered by branches of the military (U.S. Military Academy, U.S. Air Force Academy, U.S. Naval Academy, U.S. Coast Guard Academy, U.S. Merchant Marine Academy).

Simplified Needs Test: An alternate method of calculating the Expected Family Contribution for families with adjusted gross incomes of less than $50,000, who have filed, or are eligible to file, an IRS Form 1040A or 1040EZ, or are not required to file an income tax return. Excludes all assets from consideration. *See page 109*

Special Allowance: The payment the federal government provides to lenders to bring total interest rates up to market value; acts as an incentive to lending institutions to offer loans in the Federal Family Education Loan programs.

Specialized Training For Army Reserve Readiness (STARR): An educational program sponsored by the Army Reserve whereby the Reserve pays all education-related expenses for Reservists who train in selected medical specialties at their local colleges. *See page 145*

Statement of Educational Purpose: Statement signed by the student financial aid recipient indicating his/her agreement to use all financial aid funds awarded for educational or educationally related purposes only. Included as part of the FAFSA.

Student Aid Report (SAR): The official notification sent to a student as a result of the Central Processing System (CPS) receiving an applicant record (via FAFSA) for the student. The SAR summarizes applicant information, an Expected Family Contribution for the student, and displays other special messages related to the students application. In some instances the SAR may need to be submitted to the financial aid office at the school the student plans to attend, but only if the school requests it. *See Institutional Student Information Record (ISIR). See page 105*

Student Budget: *See Cost of Attendance.*

Student Contribution: A quantitative estimate of the student's ability to contribute to postsecondary expenses for a given year.

Subsidy: The money the federal government uses to help underwrite student aid programs; primarily refers to government payments to lenders of the in-school interest on Federal Stafford Loans.

Taxable Income: Income earned from wages, salaries, and tips, as well as interest income, dividend income, business or farm profits, and rental or property income.

Title IV Programs: Those federal student aid programs authorized under Title IV of the Higher Education Act of 1965, as amended. Includes: the Federal Pell Grant, Federal Supplemental Educational Opportunity Grant, Federal Work-Study, Federal Perkins Loan, Federal Stafford Loan, Federal PLUS Loan, Federal Direct Loan, Federal Direct PLUS Loan, and LEAP. *See pages 43–56*

Tuition Payment Plans: A strategy by which payment for present costs of postsecondary education is extended into a future period of time. *See page 140*

Undergraduate Student: A student who has not achieved the level of a baccalaureate or first professional degree.

Unmet Need: The difference between a student's total cost attendance at a specific institution and the students total available resources.

Untaxed Income: All income received that is not reported to the Internal Revenue Service or is reported but excluded from taxation. Such income would include, but not be limited to, any untaxed portion of Social Security benefits, Earned Income Credit, welfare payments, untaxed capital gains, interest on tax-free bonds, dividend exclusion, and military and other subsistence and quarters allowances.

Variable Interest Rate: An interest rate on a loan that is adjusted at regular intervals such as monthly, quarterly, or yearly. Federal Stafford (Subsidized and Unsubsidized), Federal PLUS, Direct Loan (Subsidized and Unsubsidized), and Direct PLUS Loans carry variable rates that are determined annually.

Verification: The process of confirming information submitted on the FAFSA through the comparison of specified documents to the data on the output document: Student Aid Report (SAR) or ISIR. Schools must verify data for students selected by the federal Central Processing System (CPS) following procedures established by regulation. Schools may also select additional applicants to undergo the verification process.

Verification Worksheet: The document the postsecondary institution sends to the student, to be completed by the student and his or her family, and returned to the institution, to obtain documentation of the verification.

Veteran (for the purposes of determining dependency): A person who has served on active duty in the Army, Navy, Air Force, Marines, or Coast Guard, or was a cadet or midshipmen at one of the service academies (except Coast Guard), and who was discharged other than dishonorably. Veterans are considered to be independent. There is no minimum length of service requirement. *See page 75*

Veteran's Educational Benefits: Assistance programs for eligible veterans and/or their dependents for education or training. *See page 75*

Vocational Rehabilitation: Programs administered by state departments of vocational rehabilitation services to assist individuals who have a physical or mental disability that is a substantial handicap to employment. *See page 76*

William D. Ford Federal Direct Loan (Direct Loan) Program: The collective name for the Direct Loan (Subsidized and Unsubsidized), Direct PLUS Loan, and Direct Consolidation Loan Programs. Loan funds for these programs are provided by the federal government to students and parents through postsecondary institutions that participate in the program. With the exception of certain repayment options, the terms and conditions of loans made under the Direct Loan Program are identical to those made under the FFEL program. *See page 56*

State Guaranty Agencies

ALABAMA
Kentucky Higher Education
  Assistance Authority
1050 US 127 South, Suite 102
Frankfort, KY 40601-4323
(502) 696-7200, (800) 928-8926
www.kheaa.com

ALASKA
United Student Aid Funds, Inc.
PO Box 6028
Indianapolis, IN 46206-6028
(317) 849-6510, (800) 872-4768
www.usafunds.org

ARIZONA
USA Funds
PO Box 6028
Indianapolis, IN 46206-6028
(317) 849-6510, (800) 872-4768
www.usafunds.org

ARKANSAS
Student Loan Guarantee Foundation
  of Arkansas
219 South Victory Street
Little Rock, AR 72201-1884
(501) 372-1491, (800) 622-3446
www.slgfa.org

CALIFORNIA
California Student Aid Commission
PO Box 419026
Rancho Cordova, CA 95741-9026
(916) 526-8999, (888) 224-7268
www.csac.ca.gov

COLORADO
Colorado Student Loan Program
999 18th Street, Suite 425
Denver, CO 80202-2471
(303) 305-3000, (800) 727-9834
www.cslp.org

CONNECTICUT
Connecticut Student Loan Foundation
525 Brook Street
Rocky Hill, CT 06067
(860) 257-4001, (800) 237-9721
www.cslf.con

DELAWARE
American Education
  Services/PHEAA
1200 North 7th Street
Harrisburg, PA 17102-1444
(717) 257-2800, (877) 603-3010
www.aessuccess.org

DISTRICT OF COLUMBIA

American Student Assistance
330 Stuart Street
Boston, MA 02116-5292
(617) 426-9434, (800) 999-9080
www.amsa.com

FLORIDA

Bureau of Student Financial
  Assistance
Department of Education
1940 North Monroe Street, Suite 70
Tallahassee, FL 32303-4759
(850) 410-5200, (800) 366-3475
www.firn.edu

GEORGIA

Georgia Higher Education Assistance
  Corporation
2082 E Exchange Place, Suite 200
Tucker, GA 30084
(770) 724-9130; (800) 776-6878
www.gsfc.org/main.cfm

HAWAII

USA Funds
PO Box 6028
Indianapolis, IN 46206-6028
(317) 849-6510, (800) 872-4768
www.usafunds.org

IDAHO

Northwest Education Loan
  Association
190 Queen Anne North, Suite 300
Seattle, WA 98109
(206) 461-5300, (800) 562-3001
www.nela.net

ILLINOIS

Illinois Student Assistance
  Commission
1755 Lake Cook Road
Deerfield, IL 60015-5209
(847) 948-8500, (800) 899-4722
www.isac-online.org

INDIANA

USA Funds
PO Box 6028
Indianapolis, IN 46206-6028
(317) 849-6510, (800) 872-4768
www.usafunds.org

IOWA

Iowa College Student Aid
  Commission
200 10th Street, 4th Floor
Des Moines, IA 50309-3609
(515) 281-3501, (800) 383-4222
www.state.ia.us/collegeaid

KANSAS

USA Funds
PO Box 6028
Indianapolis, IN 46206-6028
(317) 849-6510, (800) 872-4768
www.usafunds.org

KENTUCKY

Kentucky Higher Education
  Assistance Authority
1050 US 127 South
Frankfort, KY 40601-4323
(502) 696-7200, (800) 928-8926
www.kheaa.com

LOUISIANA
Louisiana Office of Student Financial
  Assistance
PO Box 91202
Baton Rouge, LA 70821-9202
(504) 922-1012, (800) 259-5626
www.osfa.state.la.us

MAINE
Maine Education Assistance Division
  Finance Authority of Maine
5 Community Drive
Augusta, ME 04332-0949
(207) 623-3263, (800) 228-3734
www.famemaine.com

MARYLAND
USA Funds
PO Box 6028
Indianapolis, IN 46206-6028
(317) 849-6510, (800) 872-4768
www.usafunds.org

MASSACHUSETTS
American Student Assistance
330 Stuart Street
Boston, MA 02116-5292
(617) 426-9434, (800) 999-9080
www.amsa.com

MICHIGAN
Michigan Higher Education
  Assistance Agency
PO Box 30047
Lansing, MI 48909 -7547
(517) 373-0760, (800) 642-5626
www.michigan.gov/mistudentaid

MINNESOTA
Great Lakes Higher Education
  Corporation
P.O. Box 7658
2401 International Lane
Madison, WI 53704
(608) 246-1800, (800) 236-5900
www.glhec.org

MISSISSIPPI
USA Funds
PO Box 6028
Indianapolis, IN 46206-6028
(317) 849-6510, (800) 872-4768
www.usafunds.org

MISSOURI
Missouri Student Assistance Resource
  Service
3515 Amazonas Drive
Jefferson City, MO 65109
(573) 751-3940, (800) 473-6757
www.cbhe.state.mo.us

MONTANA
Montana Guaranteed Student Loan
  Program
P.O. Box 203101
Helena, MT 59620-3101
(406) 444-6594, (800) 537-7508
www.mgslp.state.mt.us

NEBRASKA
Nebraska Student Loan Program
PO Box 82507
Lincoln, NE 68501-2507
(402) 475-8686, (800) 735-8778
www.nslp.org

NEVADA
USA Funds
PO Box 6028
Indianapolis, IN 46206-6028
(317) 849-6510, (800) 872-4768
www.usafunds.org

NEW HAMPSHIRE
New Hampshire Higher Education
  Assistance Foundation
PO Box 877
4 Barrell Court
Concord, NH 03302
(603) 225-6612, (800) 525-2577
www.nhheaf.org

NEW JERSEY
New Jersey Higher Education Student
  Assistance Authority
P.O. Box 540
Trenton, NJ 08625-0540
(609) 588-3214, (800) 792-8670
www.hesaa.org

NEW MEXICO
New Mexico Student Loan Guarantee
  Corporation
3900 Osuna NE
Albuquerque, NM 87199-2230
(505) 345-8821, (800) 279-3070
www.nmslgc.org

NEW YORK
New York State Higher Education
  Services Corporation
99 Washington Avenue
Albany, NY 12255
(518) 473-7087, (800) 697-4372
www.hesc.com

NORTH CAROLINA
North Carolina State Education
  Assistance Authority
PO Box 13663
Research Triangle Park, NC 27709
(800) 549-8614
www.ncseaa.edu

NORTH DAKOTA
Student Loan Program of North
  Dakota (Guarantor)
Bank of South Dakota
PO Box 5524
Bismarck, ND 58506-5524
(701) 328-5754, (800) 472-2166
www.mystudentloanonline.com/
index.asp

OHIO
Great Lakes Higher Education
  Corporation
2401 International Lane
PO Box 7858
Madison, WI 53704
(608) 246-1800, (800) 236-5900
www.glhec.org

OKLAHOMA
Oklahoma Guaranteed Student Loan
  Program
PO Box 3000
Oklahoma City, OK 73101-3000
(405) 234-4300, (800) 442-8642
www.ogslp.org

OREGON
Oregon Student Assistance
  Commission
1500 Valley River Drive, Suite 100
Eugene, OR 97401
(541) 687-7375, (800) 452-8807
www.osac.state.or.us

PENNSYLVANIA

American Education
  Services/PHEAA
1200 North 7th Street
Harrisburg, PA 17102-1444
(717) 257-2800, (877) 603-3010
www.aessuccess.org

RHODE ISLAND

Rhode Island Higher Education
  Assistance Authority
560 Jefferson Boulevard
Warwick, RI 02886
(401) 736-1100, (800) 922-9855
www.riheaa.org

SOUTH CAROLINA

South Carolina Student Loan
  Corporation
P.O. Box 210219
Suite 200, Interstate Center
Columbia, SC 29221
(803) 798-0916, (800) 347-2752
www.slc.sc.edu

SOUTH DAKOTA

Education Assistance Corporation
115 1st Avenue, SW
Aberdeen, SD 57401
(605) 225-6423, (800) 592-1802
www.eac-easci.org

TENNESSEE

Tennessee Student Assistance
  Corporation
404 James Robertson Parkway
Parkway Towers, Suite 1950
Nashville, TN 37243-0820
(615) 741-1346, (800) 342-1663
www.state.tn.us/tsac

TEXAS

Texas Guaranteed Student Loan
  Corporation
PO Box 201725
Austin, TX 78720-1725
(512) 219-5700, (800) 845-6267
www.tgslc.org

UTAH

Utah Higher Education Assistance
  Authority
Triad 3, Suite 550
Salt Lake City, UT 84180-1205
(801) 321-7200, (800) 418-8757
www.uheaa.org

VERMONT

Vermont Student Assistance
  Corporation
Champlain Mill, PO Box 2000
Winooski, VT 05404-2601
(802) 655-9602, (800) 642-3177
www.vsac.org

VIRGINIA

Educational Credit Management
  Corporation (Virginia)
7325 Beaufont Springs Drive,
Suite 200
Richmond, VA 23225
(804) 267-7100, (888) 775-3262
www.ecmc.org

WASHINGTON

Northwest Education Loan
  Association
190 Queen Anne North, Suite 300
Seattle, WA 98109
(206) 461-5300, (800) 562-3001
www.nela.net

WEST VIRGINIA

American Education
  Services/PHEAA
1200 North 7th Street
Harrisburg, PA 17102-1444
(717) 257-2800, (877) 603-3010
www.aessuccess.org

WISCONSIN

Great Lakes Higher Education
  Corporation
2401 International Lane
PO Box 7858
Madison, WI 53704-7858
(608) 246-1800, (800) 236-5900
www.glhec.org

WYOMING

USA Funds
PO Box 6028
Indianapolis, IN 46206-6028
(317) 849-6510, (800) 872-4768
www.usafunds.org

20 Questions Every Parent and Student Should Ask

Is it common practice to apply individual cost of attendance adjustments for students and families when requested?

What is your policy regarding "projected year income"?

What is the minimum course load required to maintain grants?

What is the school's policy on exceptions to a minimum credit load based on health or academic reasons?

May I meet with a financial aid counselor today?

Do you consider stepparents' income when analyzing an application for aid?

Do you consider an ex-spouse's income for institutional financial aid consideration?

How much grant assistance do you give a family that has been determined to have no expected family contribution?

Do you leave unmet need in your financial aid package?

What is the average debt burden of those students who graduate, and what is the average time it takes to graduate?

Does your grant aid to freshmen remain constant for their remaining three years?

Do you provide aid for summer school?

Will an outside scholarship reduce my aid award, especially my institutional grants or scholarships?

Is my institutional scholarship renewable?

Can lost scholarship eligibility be reinstated?

How long will it take to become a state resident? Do you have tuition reciprocity agreements?

How many job opportunities are there on campus?

Will my on- or off-campus job earnings affect my grant eligibility?

Does the college establish partnerships with lenders that offer student and parent discounts on loans?

Will the school package loans in order to accommodate emerging loan forgiveness programs?

FINANCIAL AID COUNTDOWN CALENDAR

Junior Year—Fall

Now is the time to get serious about the colleges in which you are interested. Meet with the guidance office to help you narrow down your choices. Hopefully by the spring, your list will have about five to ten solid choices. College visits are always a great idea-remember this will be the place you spend the next four years, so check out the campus early.

$ Register for the PSAT.

$ Check out local financial aid nights in the area. Be sure to attend these invaluable sessions, especially if this is the first time the family is sending someone off to college. Try to learn the financial aid lingo. Get some of the literature available and start to familiarize yourself with the various programs.

$ Take the PSAT/NMSQT in November.

$ Do some Web browsing. There are many great free scholarship search engines available. Now is the time to see if you might qualify for scholarships.

$ Have your parents check with their employers and church and fraternal organizations for possible scholarship opportunities.

$ Check with your guidance office for the qualifications and deadlines of local awards.

Junior Year—Winter

$ Keep checking for scholarships. Remember that this is the one area over which you have control. The harder you work, the better your chances for success.

$ Register and study for the SAT (I and II). Most college-controlled scholarship programs count the SATs heavily in their decision process. The SAT is definitely not a test that you can cram for the night before. Invest in a comprehensive test-prep guide. Using a study guide will help you get an idea of your math and verbal strengths and weaknesses. Start to schedule a little extra time to study the areas that give you problems.

Junior Year—Spring

$ Spring Break-a great time to visit colleges. Do you have a top ten list? Start narrowing your list down.

$ Review the requirements for local scholarships. What do you need to do now and this summer to improve your chances?

$ Take the SATs.

$ Look for a summer job, especially one that might tie in with your college plans.

Summer Months

$ It's college visit time, so load up the van! Begin to ask yourself some questions: Is this where I see myself getting my undergraduate degree? Can I adjust to the seasons, the town surrounding the campus, the distance from home, the college size?

Senior Year—Fall

$ Can you get your list down to five choices? Once you get focused on your five choices, make a list of what each college requires for admission and financial aid. Be sure your list prominently shows all deadlines.

$ Which colleges require the Profile application? Many private colleges use this form for institutional aid. You need to file this comprehensive form in late September or early October.

$ Get your scholarship applications filed by the published deadline. Remember, you have three sources: parent sources (employer, religious, fraternal), high school (local awards from PTA, Kiwanis, Lions Club, etc.), and Web-based search engines.

$ If planning to retake the SAT, be sure to register now.

$ You and your parents must attend a financial aid night presentation. Some of these sessions offer help in completing forms, while others offer a broader view of the process. Contact the presenter (usually a local college professional) to be sure you are getting the information you need.

Senior Year—Winter

$ Get the Free Application for Federal Student Aid (FAFSA). This is the key form for financial aid for all schools across the country. Remember, watch your deadlines, but do not file before January 1. Be sure to keep a copy of the form, whether you file electronically or with the paper form. Got some questions? Call the local financial aid office. Also, many states have special call-in programs in January and February.

$ As the letters of admission start to arrive, the financial aid award letters should be right behind. The important question for parents: What is the bottom line? Remember, aid at a lower-cost state school will be less than a higher-cost private college. But what will you be required to pay? This can be confusing, so watch for gift aid (scholarships and grants), student loans, and parent loans. The school with the lowest sticker price (tuition, fees, room, and board) might not be the cheapest when you factor in the aid package.

Senior Year—Spring

$ Still not sure where to go? The financial aid package at your top choice just not enough? Call the financial aid office and the admissions office. Talk it over. While schools don't like to bargain, they are usually willing to take a second look, especially for the high achievers.

$ By May 1, you must make your final decision. Notify the college and find out what to do next. Tell the other colleges you are not accepting their offers of admission and financial aid.

Summer

$ Time to crunch the numbers. Parents, get information from the college on the estimated charges. Deduct the aid package, and then plan for how you will pay the out-of-pocket expenses. Contact the college financial aid office for the best parental loan program.

Don't forget: You need to reapply for aid every year!

NOTES

NOTES

High school has prepared you for college, but are you prepared for financial independence?

Visit **CNN money™**

at

www.money.com

Handling your own money can be tricky. Fortunately, there's Money 101 from CNN/Money; a set of online lessons covering everything from the basics of banking, to making a budget, to buying a car. You can even track your own portfolio of stocks (even if it's just for fun). Start by going to www.money.com.

▸ Home
News
Markets & Stocks
Commentary
Technology
Personal Finance

CNN money™
Invest In Yourself

Retirement
Mutual Funds
Money 101
Money's Best
Your Portfolio
Calculators

AOL Keyword: Money

© and TM 2002. Cable News Network L.P. LLLP. An AOL Time Warner Company. All Rights Reserved.

COPYRIGHT

American Education Services (AES) is a not-for-profit, multifaceted financial aid services organization that harnesses the power of technology and innovation to better serve students, families, schools, and lenders throughout the nation.

Over the past 37 years, we have grown from a small student loan guarantor with a guaranty volume of only 4,600 loans into one of the nation's largest, full-service financial aid services providers. Today, we manage more than $35 billion in total assets and serve nearly 4 million students nationally through our guaranty, servicing, and financial aid processing systems. The funds generated from our extensive operations are used to improve higher education opportunities and lower the cost of financial assistance for students and families while streamlining the entire process for the financial aid community.

This compact disc is the property of the American Education Services (AES), which retains sole ownership rights in the contents. Neither this compact disc nor any of the information contained within can be sold, assigned, transferred or conveyed to any third party without the express written consent of AES.

Users should be aware that the examples provided are solely for the purpose of illustrating how certain financial aid calculations are made. Users should not rely upon the data or the results of such examples. AES expressly disclaims any responsibility for the accuracy of such examples.

SYSTEM REQUIREMENTS FOR WINDOWS PC

Windows® 98/NT/ME/2000/XP, Pentium 233mhz, 64 MB RAM, 8x CD-ROM, 800x600x16 bit color display.

TO RUN ON WINDOWS PC

Insert CD-ROM and wait for autorun to start the program. If the program does not appear, click "Start" then select "Run." Click "Browse" and select the CD_ROM drive, click on the PC folder then double click on aes.exe.

MINIMUM SYSTEM REQUIREMENT FOR MACINTOSH

Power PC 233mhz, MAC OS 9.1, 64 MB RAM, 8x CD-ROM, 800x600x16 bit color display.

TO RUN ON MACINTOSH

Insert CD-ROM and wait for autorun to start the program. If the program does not appear, double click on the AES icon on your desktop.